'Take, oh take me as I am,
Summon out what I shall be.
Set your seal upon my heart,
And live in me.'

- John Bell

## NOTE

Paula Grieg is writing under a false name to protect the privacy of her family, whose lives have already been adversely affected as a result of her Gender Dysphoria. All names, places and place names are false. Any resemblance to anyone living or dead is purely coincidental.

# ACKNOWLEDGEMENTS

With gratitude to my three beloved children, of whom I am immensely proud. They had to share so much of my burden and did so as best they could.

Thanks to my ex-wife, who will always have a special place in my heart; to my friends who stood by me when others walked away—you know who you are.

To my friend, Sr X, a kind and spiritual former colleague whom I will sorely miss and from whom I learned humility.

To all who made even a small contribution during my journey of self-discovery; thank you.

My gratitude is also extended to all at Maverick House who have supported me, and particularly to Lisa Coen, my editor, who patiently persevered with me and helped to shape my manuscript into the book it is now.

Finally I must acknowledge that writing truthfully about my past may cause some unintended pain to those who shared much of my life, but a memoir is either truthful or it is no longer a memoir, and my life never was a fairytale; the truth is the truth even if it is at times uncomfortable.

# DEDICATION

This book is dedicated to all the trans-women and men whose lives were diminished by prejudice, and it is written in the hope that children born today with Gender Dysphoria will have an easier passage through life in a more enlightened age.

# FOREWORD

My name is Paula Grieg. I have three children and no stretch-marks. Therein lies the story of my life; a life of inner conflicts and contradictions.

My early life, childhood and adolescence were spent in Germany, a country to which I am now bound only by memories, since almost all my family there have vanished.

I first became aware of my gender ambiguity before I reluctantly left Germany for a new life in Ireland, though at the time I had no clear idea what this meant or where it would lead.

In Ireland I fell in love, married and started a family; raising those same dearly loved three children. My career took off and I built an existence. Those who looked on might have thought I had it all, but everything I built always stood on shaky foundations, because at the very heart of it I was not who I seemed to be.

Progressively I realised that I needed to acknowledge my true self or I would never find peace within myself. But that personal inner peace came at a high price—the disintegration of family, the loss of friends, home, career and status, and once more, emigration.

Both my career and my thirst for knowledge of other places and other people have led me through five continents and more than 50 countries. They have given me a broad and tolerant outlook on diversity in every sense, while my life in two genders has given me unusual personal insights available to few. But it is also true that the more I travelled, the more I have become displaced and lost all sense of home.

This book is the telling of an unusual story. Writing it helped me to make sense of my life and I hope it will reduce barriers by helping others to understand the challenges faced by transsexuals and to realise that transsexuals can and do lead normal lives.

I remain hopeful that there is another chapter to be written, entitled, 'The Leaving of No-Man's-Land,' where, through finding love once more, I will also find that elusive sense of home and belonging, and can then look back at my life with a new perspective.

# PART 1

## GERMANY

# CHAPTER 1

## ROOTS

Europe as we know it today has been shaped by many wars and conquests. Over the centuries empires were built and lost by armies of the mostly poor for the benefit of the feudal few. One particularly dark and bloody period of European history became known as the 30-Year War. Rather than a continuous war, it was a period of many skirmishes, a trial of strength between the old establishment supporting the Pope and Holy Roman Empire on one side and the forces of the Reformation led by King Gustav-Adolph of Sweden on the other side. When the guns finally fell silent in 1648 with the signing of the Treaty of Westphalia, much of medieval Europe lay in ruins, ravaged by the twin scourges of war and bubonic plague, then commonly known as the Black Death.

When the wars finally ended, many of the ordinary foot soldiers and mercenaries who had fought on both sides found themselves displaced far from their homelands; too poor, too sick or too weary to return to their homes from where they had set out many years before. My paternal ancestor was such a soldier, a low ranking officer of the

Swedish army who settled in the benign climate of the Moselle Valley in the Palatinate region of south-west Germany. Today Rhineland-Palatinate is one of the Länder, which make up the Federal German Republic, but in the 17th century what is today's Germany was then a mosaic of many rival principalities. Still today my family name, which was Germanised from its original Swedish, is popular in the Moselle Valley.

My father spent many years of tedious and elaborate research to trace his roots. Sadly, all his work and accumulated documentation went up in smoke, lost in the ruins of his parent's home during one of two major Allied bombing raids on the city of my birth, on 30 May and on 25 June, 1943.

My maternal ancestors on the other hand were from the Rhineland. Looking at copies of old certificates of births, deaths, christenings and marriages passed on to me by an aunt who recently died at the age of 82, one can find among them vintners, farmers, reed-thatchers and members of other trades, who have long vanished. Among a nation whose people are often seen as rather dour, people from the Rhineland are generally known as fun loving and jovial, and especially at carnival time, they know how to enjoy themselves. It is with a mixture of historical curiosity and a considerable amount of unease that I look at these old documents, which had to be procured by my maternal grandparents to prove their Aryan descent—a sinister sign of the time. Each document is a copy of the original certificate going back to as far as the mid-19th century, but now emblazoned with the insignia of the spread-winged eagle atop the swastika.

These are my roots: paternal descendants of Protestant Scandinavian war emigrants, with rural Catholic stock on the maternal side. The cold north on the one hand and the warm climate of the Rhine Valley on the other; Protestant and Catholic, a bit of this and a bit of that.

# CHAPTER 2

## BIRTH

It was on 25 September 1950 that my mother gave birth to her second child. The doctors pronounced the second-born to be healthy and, in line with the physical evidence presented, declared the child to be a boy. If only they could have known.

My birth sign, therefore, is Libra, whose traits are supposedly well-balanced. Was I to become a well-balanced individual, a bridge-builder? Or simply balanced by the chip on both shoulders?

Regardless of what I was to become, I appeared that day to be born a boy, and went on to have an ordinary childhood similar to most young boys growing up at that time. I was to suffer bumps and bruises, find wonder in frogs and tadpoles, and spend my money on sweets. But to understand how later events would shape me as a person, I have to recall those earliest days.

In some ways it was a miracle that I arrived at all, my family history being complicated and touched more than once by fate. My birth appears to have been quite uneventful—I weighed in at well over nine pounds—but

I was lucky to have been born so healthy. My mother had contracted TB, which left her with a large hole in one lung, before she was married. This required intensive treatment followed by many months of recuperation in hospital. It made for a very difficult and life-threatening pregnancy.

Against the odds she survived and my father is convinced to this day that his encouragement and moral support got her through the worst and helped to miraculously close the hole in her lung. My mother survived, but her life was always blighted as a consequence of the disease. She never had more than one lung functioning at a time and even that not as well as it should have. She frequently suffered with bouts of severe breathing difficulties. Years of living with a weakened respiratory system would eventually lead to her untimely death at the age of 62 in 1987.

My birth occurred in a women's clinic right across from the one room assigned to my parents in the flat occupied by my paternal grandparents. It was still very difficult in those early post-war years to get a house, as I later learned from many letters written in 1949 by my father to my mother during her long convalescence. It took many visits to the housing authorities, endless form filling, a few useful contacts and my mother's ill health to get her on a special status list to secure a small flat.

Some months after my birth the family moved to a two-bedroom flat, a place that became home for me throughout my childhood and most of my youth. I have learned that having had the all-important first-born son, my brother, my mother would very much have liked the second to have been a girl. When I look at early pictures of myself, it is easy to believe that indeed I might have been female. My hair was long for a child of that time and a hairclip kept the troublesome fringe out of my eyes. Today I look at those pictures and dream and wonder; what if?

It is safe to assume neither I, nor indeed any of the children my father was responsible for, were in any way planned. No doubt he was particularly proud of his first-born son, as I guess all fathers generally are. It was not in fact the first child he had fathered. There had been a previous engagement, which produced my half-sister, born in 1948. Why this relationship broke down or whatever happened to the girl in question, I do not know.

Sadly I only saw my half-sister once. When I was maybe about 10 or 11 years old she came for a visit. She would have been about three years older than me and the only distinct memory I have of this visit is that it ended with trouble. This girl not only offered the first opportunity to taste one of her illicit cigarettes, but also a brief visual education about female anatomy. Unfortunately my mother found out and, needless to say, she was not too pleased. Having her stay in our house was a constant reminder of my father's previous relationship, and it can't have been easy for my mother. To find that the girl was leading her boys astray, (though it has to be said, they were more than willing), was not acceptable and the visit was cut short. Sometimes I wonder whatever became of her and where she might now live, and if she has raised her own family.

As for my older brother; my parents certainly were proud of him, particularly because of the difficulties of the birth. They named him Anthony.

For some years he has lived with his English-born wife on the continent. They too have had an odyssey, which has seen them living in Namibia, in Australia and in Indonesia before settling, for the time being, in southern Europe.

The reason for his name, which would have been strange in Germany back then, is again rooted in the war. It has to be said that, apart from this explanation for my brother's name, the war was never mentioned in our house or indeed in most German households. Millions of Germans suffered from collective amnesia following the demise of the 'Thousand Year Reich'. Even though it had thankfully fallen somewhat short of the promised thousand years, there were many things people wanted to forget. It was only decades later, when my father was in his 70s that I could bring up the subject and he would be happy to reminisce, even if only in glimpses.

My father was indoctrinated like millions of other children in the Hitler Youth and he became a willing soldier. At the time, he believed in Hitler's vision for a strong Germany and told me that he was quite prepared to fight to the bitter end. He served in the Luftwaffe as an observer in a specially equipped long distance Junkers 88 observation plane. Normally these planes were used as bombers, but some were converted for observation purposes and in such planes the observer was the officer in charge. So at a young age my father was in command of a crew. I suppose he could say that he never dropped any bombs; he only observed the damage and helped to specify the next targets.

By the end of 1944 there weren't many German planes left and not enough fuel to keep them flying either and so those who had survived and were still reasonably fit were sent to other fighting units. In the spring of 1945, as Germany was being invaded by the Red Army from the east and the Western Allies from the west, my father found himself with an infantry unit near the town of Wesel in north-west Germany, trying to prevent British forces crossing a river.

It was in this skirmish that he was hit by a machine gun bullet, which miraculously entered and exited his neck, damaging some discs, yet without severing either his spinal cord or any vital blood vessels. Nonetheless, it seemed at first that he would be paralysed or worse, but for the expert attention of a British Army medic, whose first name was that later given to my brother.

So my father saw out the rest of the war in a British Army field hospital. He got to know his lifesaver and stayed in touch with him after the war had ended. The British soldier was from Lancashire and he became the Godfather to my older brother, as well as the reason he was christened with that name. In 1964 we visited the soldier's family in Blackpool en route to our first family holiday in Ireland, but after that contact appears to have fizzled out.

If that man had not intervened when he did in those dark dying days of the war I would not have existed.

As a consequence of his war wound my father slept on double pillows throughout his life, but incidents like these make one wonder about fate. There but for a millimetre or two I would not be here to tell this story.

# CHAPTER 3

## CHILDHOOD

Here I was, born in the early 1950s, a podgy healthy baby, ready to grow up in the new Germany, young enough to have escaped the ravages of war, but old enough to remember vaguely the difficult time of its aftermath. The Federal Republic had only just come into life in the previous year of 1949 under the guidance of Konrad Adenauer, followed shortly after that by the German Democratic Republic, or since it never was democratic anyway, better known to us in the West simply as East Germany. For the next 40 years Germany was divided by the Iron Curtain. Citizens in the Federal Republic were given 50 Deutschmark each and a supposedly equal opportunity to start all over again.

My hometown, is a relatively new city, created in 1929 by the amalgamation of a number of small towns. It is a provincial city unknown to most outside Germany, with a population of about 360,000 nowadays. Located to the east of Düsseldorf and south of the old industrial heartland of the Ruhr, it took some of the heaviest damage during the war.

The city itself is mostly unremarkable. Being squeezed in by hills north and south, it runs from east to west along a tributary of the Rhine. So the city was named after the river, as is often the case.

I had a very normal upbringing here, for the most part. I appeared to be an ordinary boy who did ordinary things like getting in scrapes, paying attention to my elders, and going off on bike rides that seemed to go on all day. We were brought up in the Lutheran faith, which was somewhat surprising since my mother came from a Catholic family. I believe it was a condition of my father's family in return for their consent to the marriage. To say we were brought up in any faith is rather misleading as I can recall only two occasions when I attended church with my parents. One was the occasion of my grandfather's funeral in 1959 and once was when my mother felt the urge one Christmas to attend midnight mass in the parochial church of her youth in the picturesque village of Düssel. I remember the old whitewashed chapel sat among traditional timber-framed houses, a real Christmas card motif, especially as it was a cold snowy Christmas Eve that year. I was intrigued by the ritual of the mass, the unfamiliar smell of incense, the singing, the colour compared to the bleak black and white austerity of Protestant worship I was used to. Maybe I was already a Protestant with a Catholic heart. Unfortunately our visit was cut short as my mother almost fainted due to the heavy and unfamiliar smell of the incense.

Delving into my earliest memories, I can still vaguely recall the scarred blackened ruins of some bombed out buildings in my town. Times certainly were hard for many. My own parents had contacts with manufacturers of simple felt fabric, which was then used for making blankets and overcoats and as people slowly wanted more than the bare necessities, they came up with the idea of making berets from this material, and later slippers. My mother and my aunt, who also got involved in the business, would do all the sewing on their Singer sewing machines and my father would knock on doors of stores all over the city and beyond to get sales.

People were inventive, they worked hard to survive, to start all over again, to keep busy and not to dwell too much on dark memories. In some relatives' houses I remember the faded black and white photographs of men in uniforms, sons who had not returned from Russia and other places. There were a lot of women in black in those early days, but then of course, those scenes were repeated all over Europe. My grand aunt was a good example; I always remember her; white-haired, always dressed in black with so much sadness in her eyes. On her bedside locker stood the silver-framed pictures of her two fine looking sons in uniform. One was lost somewhere on the Eastern Front during the war and the other fell in France. My grand aunt lived to her 80s, though she became senile and so escaped her sad memories.

There would be some family get-togethers, mostly visiting either of my grandparents' houses. A visit to my father's parents was never particularly looked forward to. They had only had two children, my father and his sister, who later moved with her husband and her two sons to the Frankfurt region, which meant contact with my two cousins was limited after my early years.

My grandfather was an aloof man who had worked as an accountant's assistant. His hobbies were playing violin and bird-watching, but I cannot say that I ever really got to know him. He died from asthma in his 60s. His wife, my grandma, lived to the age of 92, but she too was not one who found the company of children easy. We would be given some board games and told to be as quiet as possible. Their flat was somewhat dark, quiet and always too tidy to be homely. Everything always had to be in its precise place.

My other grandparents were quite different. My granddad Paul, after whom I had been named, was a jovial man, who enjoyed company, a drink, a game of cards and a joke. Sadly I was not to get to know him too well, because he died at the age of 59, a victim of lung disease, but really a victim of circumstance and the times he lived in—the Great War, then the Depression, and finally World War II. In the days following the Allied Normandy landings my grandfather found himself with his comrades in a tunnel below a chateau with gas grenades slowly suffocating all around him. I have a hand-written diary of the account of his capture. It is written in the old German style in a faded American spiral-bound notebook. He wrote it on his way to captivity in the cotton fields of far away Texas. My granddad's short diary makes hard reading and shows the horror of war, irrespective of the colour of the uniform. Apart from the commanding officers who left their men to their fate before the final assault, only he and one of his comrades survived and only because the two of them, as battery commanders, had been issued with a newer type of gas mask. He mentions some of the dying comrades around him by name and I always wonder if their families ever knew their tragic end.

In spite of what life had thrown at him, my granddad remained a simple and kind man. At least that is my short memory of him. My granny Christine was also a fun-loving woman; easy going with her children and her grandchildren, she also carried the burdens of her life with dignity. She lost her beloved husband early. She suffered again terribly when the youngest of her three daughters lost her life in a car accident. Her VW skidded on an icy city street into an oncoming truck. My granddad had only lived to 59 and his youngest daughter, my aunt, had followed at just 42, but then that's life, just a transition of indeterminable duration for all of us. In her later years my granny would always be ready for a chat. She would sit for hours doing crosswords, smoking too many cigarettes and drinking black coffee.

When I last visited my home city I stood under the birch tree above my granddad's grave. In 1959 when he was placed beneath it, it was not much more than a sapling, but the very plot had been chosen because he loved birch trees. Now the fresh bright green leaves rustle under a tall mature tree. It is good to know in a way that his decaying bones have helped to give the tree its strength. There, separated by only one stranger's grave lie my two grandfathers; one gave me my surname and the other my first name, which I found I could not keep.

\*\*\*

Our family home from my early childhood to my 16th year was a two-bedroom flat on the first floor of a six-storey pre-war town house in a row of similar houses. On the ground level at the front there were two small business premises, one a hairdresser and the other a sweet shop, where I would spend much of my limited pocket money over the next few years. At the back were the cellars where we would keep coal, potatoes, assorted junk and our bicycles.

My father was always into recording the family events and it is through the old pictures that I can rekindle memories of early childhood; there are the annual pictures under the Christmas tree, with my brother and I looking up with a mixture of awe and anticipation at the candle-lit branches. Other pictures show us at Easter following the tradition of looking for hidden Easter eggs, which we foolishly thought the Easter Bunny had deposited for us. There are pictures of day trips, often to rivers or lakes, because my father would take any opportunity to do a bit of fishing. I often look at those pictures of me as a small child and I try to look into my eyes to understand my feelings and emotions at that time. I don't recall feeling that I was in any way different because I wasn't; certainly not in those years before consciousness of sexuality and gender came into play. I appeared a normal little boy who did normal 'boy' things.

From our bedroom window we could look out over the cobbled street below. In the middle were the double tracks of the tram. You could hear it coming before you saw it, because there was a slight bend in the road just below our house and if I listen really hard I can still hear that familiar squeal of metal on metal.

Across the street the houses were elegant, mostly pre-war, detached or semi-detached villas with surrounding gardens. The street was tree-lined with mature elm, beech and large chestnut trees, which supplied us with plenty of conkers in autumn. It was just a few hundred yards down our street to where it ended with a T-junction onto the city's main east-west artery road, left leading towards the city centre and right, the route for our daily walk to school. This junction would be our limit and there were a few shops and a filling station there and a lane leading to the entrance of the allotments behind our houses. There was also a red fire emergency pillar located there. One day I could not resist and activated the alarm. When the loud alarm sounded I hurriedly scampered off, hid nearby and watched in horror as the fire engine arrived within a few minutes. I was no little angel, though this frightened me more than it excited me and I never did it again.

Among the corner shops here I particularly remember the Drogerie Todt, an intriguing old-fashioned chemist with lines of glass jars with all sorts of mysterious compounds and powders, rows and rows of little metal-handled wooden drawers, big scales with all their weights lined up in ascending order and Mr Todt, with his little spectacles and white shop coat.

Across the street was another favourite shop, the bakery, where we would get fresh bread and freshly baked rolls, and sometimes there would be a treat of a confectionary or even a slice of cream cake. The smells in there really got to me, and from early on I developed a sweet tooth, something else inherited from my grandfather Paul.

I remember summers spent mostly outdoors, exploring the neighbourhood. We would walk just a short distance to a hillside farm, where we would be sent daily by my mother to buy fresh milk in a one-litre battered tin can. I recall the big sloping meadow beside the farm buildings with a single sturdy oak tree right in the middle. Once at Christmas, we got a new proper wooden sledge with metal edges and we had great fun sliding down the hillside again and again. Then a child neighbour, a year or so older than me, wanted to have a go as well and persuaded us to let him ride along with us. The sledge was really only big enough for two, but I was squeezed in the middle and off we went down the hill, a little faster with the extra weight, and a little out of control. The other boy who had insisted on steering, managed to head for the one and only big oak tree and while both he and my brother managed to throw themselves off, I hit the tree and was carried home in a bloody mess.

Winters often brought lots of snow and we would play outside until we were frozen stiff and would then howl with the pain of defrosting our fingers and toes in the warmth of the flat. But as soon as possible we would be out again.

We were encouraged to go outside as much as possible, because living in a first floor flat above a shop and below the flat of the landlady could at times be problematic. The house owner, a grumpy old Frau, lived alone, having lost her husband during the war. She threatened to have us thrown out more than once, either because she herself found our boisterous playing too noisy or because the owner of the hairdressing salon complained to her about the noise coming from above.

\*\*\*

In later years when we had bikes my brother and I would set off for longer excursions, usually unknown to my parents. One trip I remember was to another large, but sadly by then, more or less derelict country house. Though the grand house was empty and boarded up we managed to get in, and run through the empty rooms listening to the echo of our voices and our steps. I was trying hard to listen to the echo of the past. I could imagine people dining sumptuously and dancing in their fineries in the great hall. For a little while we could pretend to be the king of the castle. Even from childhood, I was fascinated by history.

My younger brother Harald was born a few years after me and naturally all attention fell on him. Looking back, I think I suffered sometimes from the in-between feeling that middle siblings experience. There was the all-important first-born son and now there was the cute little baby to be pampered, and there in the middle, was me.

Later that year, after the last carefree long summer, I started school. The first school day was a big occasion in Germany. The child would get a large, nicely decorated and sweet-filled cardboard cone and take it to school. Of course a picture of the big event would be taken for posterity. I was a small blonde child with a big grin in checked bib-trousers, proud to be ready for school.

After school we would do our homework, then some chores around the home; only then would we be allowed out to play. We hated chores at home because it would involve dusting skirting boards, sweeping floors, vacuuming, washing up and, worst of all, we often had to wash the stairs and stairwells from the ground-floor entrance of the building to the first floor.

We would watch out through two small glass panes in the entrance door to see if anyone was approaching to avoid being seen. If someone did approach, we would quickly hide around a corner by the cellar doors. We didn't think it would be good for us, as boys, to be seen washing floors, because our friends would make fun of us. Unfortunately, we had no sisters to do this and my mother would often simply not be able, because of her poor health and breathlessness. It is strange how, even then as children, we already had an inherent idea of what boys and girls 'ought' to be doing and of what constituted being male.

Another duty was polishing my father's shoes before going to bed and it had to be done right, because he would inspect them and have you do them again if they were not tip-top. We got a very small weekly allowance, which would barely cover the price for a few sweets or a comic. We would spend what little we had either in the sweet shop below us or another small stationery shop, which also sold some comics and small toys like little plastic cars. To my shame I also remember pilfering some of these little toy cars on a couple of occasions.

***

Where my father lacked any emotional warmth, he was a talented builder and decorator, but I used to dread when he would ask me for help. Invariably I would be a bundle of nerves the moment he needed me, because I never seemed to be able to do things just right for him. I cannot remember praise, but I can remember him losing his patience many times, getting angry; temper veins flaring in his face when things did not go his way.

It was during my early school years, when I was about eight years old, that one of the seminal incidents of my early youth occurred—an event that made a life-long impression on me and fractured my relationship with my father.

We had been on one of our returns from school and decided to see who could throw stones furthest across the road into the river on the far side. Though this was a main road, traffic was much lighter in those days. On our side of the road there was only a steep wooded slope and on the other side beyond the road and well below it was the river.

We tossed our stones, oblivious to our surroundings, and failed to notice an approaching VW Beetle. A stone landed on the bonnet with a thud and we ran like hell. We really hadn't intended to hit the car, but we had been careless. We knew the quickest way home and thought we had gotten away with it, but as we walked this same way every day someone must have told the driver of the car who we were and where we lived. Sometime later that afternoon the doorbell rang and a policeman appeared at our door. I can still see this giant policeman in his green uniform with the silver buttons and the somewhat frightening black Prussian style helmet that German policemen wore in those days. No protestations of innocence would suffice. We got a stern talking to from the policeman and my mother only said: 'Wait till your father gets home.'

When my father did return it did not take long for his temper to explode and I can still see the child that was me, screaming with fear and pain as he disciplined me. I was frozen with fear as my father punished me, then lifted, manhandled, me up the stairs. I was left standing there, a shivering, frightened mess; a little boy terrified by the rage and humiliated by my reaction.

That one incident scarred me more than any other and destroyed my relationship with my father forever. Only in very recent times have I made him understand the damage his temper and his harsh discipline caused me. Though I have forgiven him, I cannot forget and I regret that it has robbed us of a true understanding. He has in his way apologised, blaming his own loveless upbringing for his ways.

Of course, this has to be seen in the context of the time, a time when much harsher regimes of discipline were not unusual. I do know that my father did not set out to leave me psychologically scarred, but now fearful wariness would prove too often an obstacle to love.

\*\*\*

My mother had a knack for getting us children on holidays with all kinds of different groups; some were through the official welfare channels and others through charitable organisations. Whether my parents' primary motivation was to provide us with an adventure or to give themselves a well-deserved break from us, I am not sure, but it certainly opened new worlds for us.

Today there are only hazy memories of these vacations, but each one is remembered for different reasons. One year we went with the Catholic Caritas organisation to a convent in the town of Weert in Holland. There are two things I particularly remember about this vacation. First of all, that it was embarrassing for the two of us really, because all the other children were Catholic and we didn't know how to behave in a Catholic church.

The other was an incident which occurred there and which still angers me to this day. My brother Anthony had gotten into trouble with one of the other children. Once Anthony was caught, it was decided by the group leaders that he would be punished by the strongest boy in the group, who would give him a good hiding in front of everyone. So the kids formed a tight circle, blocking any escape route, and I can vividly remember crying and having to be restrained by the other children at the outer edge of the circle as my brother was beaten. Anthony just decided to curl up tightly and let the other boy do his worst with punches from above until the group leader decided it was enough. I felt helpless, because I could not defend my sibling, but also embarrassed and acutely humiliated because I wanted him to fight back. I think he was less bothered by the affair than I was. What angers me still is the way the people in charge dealt with this incident.

Then there was another summer vacation, when I was about eight or nine, to the East Friesian island of Norderney. It was my first seaside holiday and while the North Sea cannot offer the warm water of the Mediterranean, the less crowded sandy beaches were very pleasant indeed, especially to city children, who had not seen much of the sea at that time. However, one incident stands out from this holiday. It was my first sexual encounter of sorts.

We slept in dormitories in bunk-beds with maybe eight or ten boys to a room. Unfortunately some of the boys were further advanced with puberty than others and one evening one boy started to very publicly play with himself. Not only was he showing off, he was also trying very hard to get others to join in, and one or two others certainly did. As for me, I did not know what I should do and just wanted to hide. This was unexpected and totally unknown territory for me and I pretended to be asleep, but it gave me something to think about for a long while after that, and awoke my curiosity in sex.

One summer in the 1960s, our whole family went on what would prove to be a significant holiday to Ireland. Being in my teens, it might well be argued that childhood was behind me, but it is worth mentioning for its later consequences. My father had been involved in some business venture with someone who later set up a holiday business aimed at angling tourism specifically to Ireland, which at that time was still quite undeveloped. So that summer we set off on the long journey to Ireland by car, packed with my parents, children, luggage and fishing tackle. Of course this was a great adventure for us; the first ferry crossing, and a chance for Anthony and I to try some of our early school English. We stayed over one night in Blackpool, enjoyed the Tower and the Pleasure Beach, while my father reacquainted himself with his wartime lifesaver.

The ferry crossing from Holyhead to Ireland was then still with the old mail-boat with each vehicle being winched aboard by crane in big slings. It took about four hours to get us into Dun Laoghaire. We went up from there to the North-East first.

We spent the first two weeks within the vicinity fishing the local lakes with some success; the lakes were then quite undeveloped and certainly full of specimen fish. We also discovered that it rained a lot in Ireland, even in August, and I don't think my mother—who was certainly not in the least interested in fishing— enjoyed her holiday very much. When we boys got bored with fishing we would explore the surrounding countryside or walk into the nearby town to eat chips and take in the urban landscape that was so different from what we were used to in Germany.

There was one incident which I will always remember as it was the first time I witnessed the marvel of birth. I had strayed across some fields and heard loud and continuous shrieking coming from a nearby shed. I approached carefully, not sure of what to expect. When I peered into the open stable I saw an enormous sow lying on straw and just as I entered she commenced giving birth to her first piglet. For me as a city kid, totally ignorant even at nearly

14 about such matters, it was amazing. Before I knew it I saw the second and third piglet appearing and I wanted to run off to tell the farmer or anyone nearby that the pig was having babies. But every time I made a move to go another piglet would appear. I counted 13 little pink and bloodied piglets in the end, and counting them was not easy, because there was a right mess of umbilical cords and little curled tails and a crescendo of squeaks and squeals. Not for many years did I get another opportunity to watch the dramatic beginnings of life unfold, and then it would be the birth of my twin daughters.

We spent the last two weeks of our holiday sea fishing in Dungarvan, County Waterford, and touring some of the surrounding countryside.

So we had made acquaintance with Ireland; it was an interesting and certainly most charming country for a visitor back then. There was little fear of crime in those days; you could leave anything lying around and be sure to still find it there later. People seemed to always have time to chat and life moved at a different pace. On the downside the roads were atrocious, the variety of goods and products on offer compared to what we were used to in Germany was limited. Nowadays, of course, Ireland has made much progress. It is a modern society with much improved infrastructure and a much more urbanised society, including all the modern problems that go with it.

# Chapter 4

## Adolescence

It is maybe a moot point to try to define when childhood ends and adolescence begins, but I guess the onset of puberty, which finally leaves the innocence of childhood behind, if there is such a thing, is as good a point as any. While I can no longer recall the exact date or even exactly what age I was when my puberty began, I can all too clearly remember the defining moment, that awakening of gender, which set me off on that arduous journey which would last many years, trying to discover my true identity and my place in the world.

In the early years at home Anthony and I had shared a room, sleeping in two single beds. Later, after my younger brother's arrival and when he had outgrown his cot, a bunk-bed replaced one of those single beds and all three of us shared the room; not very spacious, but sufficient. Many have grown up in more confined circumstances. Across the corridor was a small bathroom, with an old-fashioned bathtub, a sink and an ungainly gas boiler responsible for heating all the hot water. One day it was also responsible for blowing my mother right through the closed bathroom door, thankfully without serious injury to her. It did, however, leave me with a lasting fear of gas-fired appliances.

Adjacent to our bedroom was the sitting room or lounge, where my father had a large writing bureau in one corner. At Christmas time the tree would be placed there, but otherwise the lounge was mostly out of bounds for us. The last door at the top end of the corridor led to my parents' bedroom. If the lounge was out of bounds, my parents' bedroom was even more so and we would never enter without knocking if my parents were inside.

'Out of bounds' is of course an irresistible invitation to any child and I remember my older brother and I sampling a little of the alcohol in the drinks cabinet, even being wise enough to add a little water to keep the level of the bottles right, a trick probably repeated by my own children many years later.

As both my parents worked throughout those years, my father in a variety of jobs and my mother more on a casual part-time basis, there were times when we would be alone even at a surprisingly young age. This was not by choice but economic necessity. My father never seemed to progress in any occupation, which was not because he was not capable, but he would usually end up telling his bosses how to run their business and it would not be long before he would find himself in another job.

My mother did things like in-store product demonstrations and I remember her working for companies like Ovaltine and Felicitas, which I believe paid her only on a commission basis. In later years she earned an extra income by making and selling very nicely dressed dolls, which she made from fabric off-cuts. She really was very skilled at it.

Anyway, back to my impending onset of puberty and the beginnings of adolescence. One day I found myself alone in the flat without my brothers, which would not have happened very often.

An unusual and inexplicable restlessness came over me and somehow I felt drawn to my parents' bedroom, to the secrets it might hide. A little unsure, I stood in front of the pair of large bright wooden wardrobes. From occasional observation I knew that the one on the right held my mother's things and the one on the left my father's. Ignoring the latter, I tentatively tried the key in the lock of my mother's wardrobe, unlocked it and gently opened the double doors.

A row of shelves on the right within the wardrobe held all my mother's underwear, neatly sorted into knickers, bras, stockings, suspenders, petticoats, girdles and whatever would have been fashionable in the late 50s and early 60s. There I stood, uncertain about what was happening to me, not knowing why I felt the way I felt, afraid of being caught right there, a little boy standing there trying to imagine wearing some of his mother's clothes, something any mum's little daughter might try and feel none the worse for it, but why me?

For long moments I stood and gazed, suspended between fear and curiosity, before that curiosity gradually overcame the fear. Carefully, I took one of the items, a nice bright pair of soft cotton knickers; I just felt the softness and then I wanted to know how they would feel if I wore them. Still in a daze, I discarded my clothes and stood there naked, shivering with either cold or fear or excitement or all of those, and I put on the soft knickers. They felt so much nicer than anything I would usually have to wear.

Not satisfied, I took out a pair of stockings. It took me a while to figure out how best to get them straight, all the while fearful of tearing them. Again I paused and considered abandoning this quest, but I could not yet tear myself away. I felt compelled at least to try on a complete set of underwear, and I wrestled for ages with the hooks of a suspender-belt, and then finally added a petticoat. I looked at the strange apparition in the large mirror. It looked all wrong and yet it felt right, it felt warm and soft and tender.

I could imagine being a girl, but why should I want to? I was a boy. But I felt this strange sensation that I was somehow opening the door to my real identity for the very first time. Before long, a trance-like state of excitement overcame me and I felt warm liquid running down my thigh.

For a few seconds I remained in my confused, excited, breathless state and then panic set in; fear of discovery. As quick as I could I undressed, cleaned up my mess and tidied everything away exactly as I had found it, double-checked once more that everything was in its place and fled the room.

Instinctively I knew that this was a special, defining moment, though what it all meant I neither knew nor could comprehend—I was frightened. Even then though, I understood that this was not what boys were meant to do, or meant to feel, and with that I also knew that I could not share this secret with anyone. So now, as I saw it, I had to keep a big dark secret and with that, my innocence was gone. From that day on I would live a lie and that lie would last for many years to come.

\*\*\*

I began to sleep fitfully, with strange dreams, waking up with the bed tossed and often with the sheet stained, something any boy would, of course, experience. There was only one problem—in my dreams I was not always a boy.

Rather, I would be just like any other girl, playing innocent games with other girls, giggling at their own little conspiracies and secrets, full of laughter, happy and at ease in their own company and me among them, accepted as just one of them, part of their group. If I could recall one of these dreams on wakening I would lie there trying to hold onto it and then have to let go, the feelings of contentment giving way to confusion and loneliness.

All this coincided with the end of my four years of primary school and soon I would be due to start at secondary school. It would prove to be a difficult time for me. For some reason my parents insisted that I should go to a school with heavy emphasis on science and classic languages.

It was an all-boys school and I was shy and going through a difficult and confusing phase. Somehow I could neither get into some of the new subjects, particularly algebra and Latin, nor even find any liking for them. However, I did well at German and liked learning English, and even loved history and geography. Latin and maths were key subjects I really struggled with. I just about managed to scrape through the first year.

Between getting to and from school, doing homework, still doing our chores at home and also doing a paper round to earn some pocket money, there was not a lot of spare time, but we tried. Both my brother Anthony and I had joined a local YMCA group where we went one evening a week. Sometimes they arranged some special do for a weekend as well as some summer camps.

We started listening to a new kind of music around then. Our favourites were The Rolling Stones, but also The Kinks, The Hollies, Eric Burton and the Animals and anything rock and roll—the 1960s were here. But despite all the distractions, I was still very confused.

When a chance presented itself and I would find myself alone in the house, I would invariably be drawn to my mother's wardrobe, where I would go further with dressing up. These would be treasured moments, but invariably those moments would be followed by feelings of guilt and confusion. Nobody knew what I was doing.

There were occasions when I came very close to getting caught, but it never happened and sometimes I wonder how things would have turned out if I had been found out. But it would be wishful thinking, knowing my parents and the times we lived in, to think it would have helped me in any way. There were these strong urges to be a girl and yet it was also a time when I became infatuated for the first time with a girl.

Her name was Angelica; she was blonde, small and slim, and always nicely dressed in bright colours. I used to see her on the train every day. She would usually be with a few friends and I never really worked up the courage to say much more than hello, and even that took a long time. Later I found out where she lived and cycled around her estate on the weekend on the off-chance that I might meet her. If I didn't I would be disappointed and if I did I would cycle past a few times and then I might just say hello. Looking back now it seems extraordinary that I was so shy, but I cannot really say whether I looked at Angelica as the girl I wanted to have as my girlfriend, or as the girl I would have loved to be.

I did not make any close friends among classmates. It was not that I was disliked or picked on or bullied; I just found it very hard to let others get in close. I was different, I carried a secret, and it always prevented me from being totally at ease and happy with myself.

Most of my life has been spent on the periphery, afraid of the dazzling lights of centre stage, which might expose my innermost secrets. It reminds me of the rhyming refrain of a German children's song: '*Ach wie gut, daß keiner weiß, daß ich Rumpelstilzchen heiß*,' which, loosely translated is: 'Oh how good that no one knows, that my real name is Rumpelstilzchen.'

Yes, I played the part of the young boy Paul, doing all the things expected of young boys, but deep inside me lived someone else, buried alive, screaming silently sometimes, wishing to be released like the genie from the lamp and yet terrified of the consequences if the genie was released. But what could I do? Where could I turn? There was no information and there were no support systems back then for something like this.

\*\*\*

My effort at school did not show much sign of improvement. I had rubbed up the chemistry teacher the wrong way, which wasn't hard to do. He was an abrasive man with round-rimmed glasses, thick as bottle ends, and I showed little interest for his experiments. Latin was—well just all Latin to me and with maths, or more specifically algebra, I was also labouring, though I did okay with everything else. When it looked like I might fail my second year and my parents realised that I had lost all interest in school, they decided to let me leave.

After some debating of what I could and should do I was taken on as an apprentice by a gentleman who then ran a chain of travel companies in the city. Even then I knew that I wanted to see more of the world and I reckoned, and not without reason, that I would be able to further my ambitions in that regard by working within the travel industry.

I can still remember getting my first opportunity for a free trip by train to Brussels. I was so excited that I couldn't sleep at first, then slept through the alarm and missed the train. Nonetheless I settled well enough into my apprenticeship and also did well at the Trades School I attended twice weekly.

The first year was typically basic apprenticeship stuff; looking after internal mail distribution, updating the reference libraries, which was very different in this pre-computer age, keeping brochures neat and stocked up on the shelves.

Then I learned how to use all kinds of timetables and how to issue bus, train and air tickets. After some time learning the basics at the main branch, I was transferred to smaller branch offices where I worked entirely with women. Ever since I have found that I work very well with women.

Throughout this time I remained shy though, and never had any girlfriends. I did go to some parties at friends' houses and I did fancy some girls, but I never quite knew where to go from there; certain male instincts seemed to be lacking. There were girls I liked, but as with Angelica a few years before, I never was quite sure whether I wanted to be with them or just be them. I did enrol in dancing school when I was about 16 or 17, got on well with my dancing partner, and learned the waltz, the foxtrot, the rumba and the tango, but beyond that nothing developed.

Anthony and I went to occasional parties at friends' houses, though they would primarily be Anthony's friends. We would listen to the Rolling Stones and feel rebellious. One summer in the late 1960s, we went on a visit to Amsterdam for the weekend, because that was a groovy place to be then, the centre of 'Flower Power' in Europe. There we could sing along with Scott McKenzie and dream of San Francisco, wearing flowers in our hair and our peace badges and hope to change the world. Of course we didn't, but just then for a year or two there seemed to be real possibilities. It was an idealistic time; the air could be heavy with the scent of hash one moment or teargas the next. There were student riots in Europe. In Germany there was the Great Coalition, which led to the setting up of the APO student movement from which no doubt more sinister elements emerged.

Within a year Martin Luther King and Bobby Kennedy would be dead, the Russians would have crushed the Prague Spring with their tanks and somehow all of the idealism seemed to evaporate. And against that backdrop I would lose my country, my friends and my home, and have my life thrown into even more turmoil.

\*\*\*

Sometime in the late 1960s my father decided to set up his own niche business within the building trade. He had been employed with a specialist contractor working with damp proofing systems and he thought he had learned enough to do it cheaper and better. So he set up his own business, taking one or two others with him from the old firm. As a further sideline a large plastics processor and extruder was purchased. This was then tooled up to produce plastic skirting boards in high volume.

At first all seemed to go well enough. My father bought a new turquoise green metallic two-litre Ford. My mother also now had a little sports car. Then he persuaded the owner of a large edge of town bungalow to divide the house, convert the loft in one half of the house and then rent this now semi-detached dormer bungalow to him.

We now seemed to have arrived, moving from our first floor flat, our home of some 15 years, to a dormer bungalow with a spacious garden surrounded by green countryside.

My father's dream of independence was not to last. Everything seemed to unravel quite quickly—the business collapsed and was put into liquidation. Things didn't look good. Under German company laws, my mother, registered as the company secretary, would have been personally liable for considerable debts, which would have been clawed back from her future earnings.

This final chapter in our lives in Germany was also marred by strains in my parents' marriage, but as everything collapsed around us, my father planned a new life for us in Ireland, where he felt there would be new opportunities.

It must have been very hard for my poor mother, leaving her own ageing mother, her sisters and friends, at a time when she was in poor health and without a word of English. I think that had it not been for the financial implications, which my mother would have faced if staying in Germany, my parents might well have split at that time.

Then, incredibly, my mother became pregnant. It was considered a good omen for a new beginning, but a child could not have been conceived at a worse time. Financial security was all but gone and a child seldom saves a rocky marriage. My mother was in poor health and would give birth in a foreign land at over 43 years of age.

I also found this new life traumatic. It was quickly agreed that my brother Anthony could stay to continue his studies as he would be old enough to fend for himself. But I was still only 17 and though I begged and pleaded to stay to finish my travel agent apprenticeship and to live with my granny, I was not allowed to do so. Without any proper research my father insisted it would be no problem to get into a travel agency near where we would live in Ireland, which proved utter nonsense as it turned out.

And so my father set off with my now 12 year-old brother to prepare the ground, to find a suitable and cheap property and find some work that would support us. As soon as all this was accomplished, my mother, by now heavily pregnant, was to follow with me.

I was by now resigned to having to go with them, as I could not support myself with my apprentices' wages and no place to stay. By early June my father informed us that he had found this wonderful empty country house with ideal potential to convert into a guesthouse for fishermen.

So one day the three of us, that is my mother, my as yet unborn sister and I set off on the long journey to Ireland in my mother's small red two-seater NSU Sports Prince. Now about eight months pregnant, my mother barely fitted into the car; getting in and out was a real struggle for her and she would have to do all the driving.

We took a night ferry from Amsterdam to Immingham, crossed the UK and two days later took the Mail Boat from Holyhead to Dun Laoghaire, south of Dublin, Ireland.

A huge chapter of my life was over; I was an unwilling emigrant for the first, though not the last time in my life. Though I learned to love Ireland in the following years, a part of me forever stayed in Germany.

It was not my choice to leave my homeland, but a decision forced upon me at the time, and it has always left me with a feeling of upheaval and rootlessness. That feeling was only going to get stronger as time went by.

# Part 2

# Ireland

# CHAPTER 5

## FIRST IMPRESSIONS

It is not easy for me to recall those early days in Ireland. There certainly was an array of mixed emotions; the excitement of being part of something new and strange, tempered by the knowledge that this would replace the known and trusted surroundings left behind. There was the fear of the unknown, worry about our precarious financial situation, concern about my mother's poor health and the looming birth, and apprehension about our poor means of communicating. Not to mention my confusion over what was going on within me.

My father spoke reasonably good English, though to this day even after decades in Ireland, his accent can still be easily identified as German. My mother spoke practically no English and would never really master it. I too had only very rudimentary English skills and what little I knew often drew blank expressions in response, as the idiom of my school English was generally not compatible with the real language as spoken in the rural parts of the area in which we settled. That would not prove a stumbling block for long though; learning a language while relatively young in the area where it is spoken soon makes for fluency, even with the right accent.

Having read the letters in which my father wrote lyrically about our wonderful new home, setting eyes on it for the first time was a shock for my mother and I. No doubt the place had a certain charm, an air of mystery and sense of history about it. For anyone with the right spare capital to hire the necessary skilled and unskilled labour and/or the right kind of power tools, it presented an excellent opportunity. We, however, did not have any capital and so we had to do largely without the power tools and we would also be the labour; we—that is my father, my brother who had turned 13, and me. My mother, in poor health and due to give birth soon, would hardly be able to do much hard grafting other than look after the new arrival and do some cooking and light housework.

You could see that it had once been a great house and you could imagine the yard bustling with activity, noises and smells of livestock, chickens, horses, dogs and cats, filled with all the machinery and paraphernalia of a busy working farm. You could imagine the smell of fresh laundry fluttering in the breeze on the washing line. You could imagine, but the reality was very different.

The place looked quite desolate—somewhere that had served its purpose and was now long past its time. The surrounding site was unkempt and overgrown; weeds and brambles had intertwined everywhere with the now choked-looking rhododendrons and shrubs. The main house and adjoining outbuildings had shed the top layer of their lime plaster and whitewash in large areas and now the buildings looked spotty and damp. The window frames were rotten in many places and beyond repair. The long building to the right, which, going by the layout and the still pungent horse-manure, had served as horse stables, was in the best condition as it was built with solid dressed sandstone.

Beech Mount House was built some 300 years ago, originally, so we were told, as a hunting lodge for some local squire. Then it was in the hands of the same family for some 240 years and became the largest farm in the area. Later, when there was no remaining male heir to pass the house and land onto, the farm was broken up and the land dispersed by the Irish Land Commission to various farmers, leaving only the tired and worn out empty old house with less than an acre to be disposed of by auction. Looking at the state of the place when we arrived, it was not surprising that there had been little interest at the auction and my father had acquired the place very cheaply.

Little did I know then that the house would cast its long shadows over my life for the next few decades; how often I wished I had never laid eyes on it, because it brought so much heartache for our family. Maybe the house should have been left to its slumber and decay, but instead a new family of invaders was to disturb its ghosts.

The usual approach to Beech Mount House was via the old coach road that wound its way through the treacherous bends in the area. It followed the wall and boundaries of the large estate belonging to a local family, members of the Anglo-Irish landowner's class. They were wealthy but often despised by those who had to pay them ground rents, which at that time would have been anyone who had property along the one half of the main street in the town.

There were many local lakes at that time which were hardly developed, but rich in fish. This is what had persuaded my father to choose this area for his angling tourism venture.

Anyone living near this spot will take it for granted, as I did when I still lived there. It is often only when you have lost something that you learn to appreciate it. In a way it summarises all that I liked about Ireland; unspoilt then, peaceful, rural and idyllic.

My association with this area would last for more than 30 years. I would own houses near this very spot on either side of the river, which marks the dividing line not only between two counties, but also the dividing line between the ancient provinces. It is strange how my life has always been in borderland, never quite belonging to either side.

For anyone coming from an urban environment in what was then the Federal Republic of Germany, to a rural setting in Ireland was a complete culture shock. West Germany in the late 1960s was among the most developed nations in Europe with one of the world's strongest economies. In contrast, Ireland in those pre-EU days was, in the context of Europe, a backwater, inward looking and wrapped up in its own history and conflicts with British policies in Ireland.

With its 3.5 million inhabitants, it was a world away from what we had been used to. The rural by-roads and even main roads were often in a terrible state, but then traffic was also very light, both in comparison to the Ireland of today and in relation to what we had been used to, living along a busy city street. There was an amazing amount of old, damaged and faulty vehicles on the road. One was liable to meet farm machinery and tractors with no lights and there seemed to be very little adherence to, or enforcement of the rules of the road. If you were unlucky enough to be stopped by a garda, you could generally talk yourself out of minor misdemeanours.

Ireland then was a charming, easy-going and laid-back country, where people took time to shoot the breeze, gossip at crossroads or on street corners, where you could leave your doors unlocked and where there was a strong sense of community, but also lots of local rivalries.

The other side of the easy-going Irish mentality was a frustrating unreliability. There were many things taken for granted in the past, which suddenly were not available locally and if a shopkeeper would promise to have something in a day or two, that could just as easily become a week or two or indeed not at all. You had to learn to improvise or to travel to one of the larger provincial towns in the hope of finding what you wanted there. This applied both to specific tools or building materials or even to groceries; for example, ground coffee was not to be had anywhere locally in those early days. It was all a bit of a culture shock for us, but we were here to stay and would have to learn to adapt.

# CHAPTER 6

## A NEW BEGINNING

Within a month of our arrival my mother went off to hospital to get ready for the birth of her fourth child. My parents had ruled out any of the local hospitals due to my mother's poor health and age and the probability of a difficult birth. So it came down to a choice between either one of the Dublin maternity hospitals and those in Northern Ireland. The distance would be similar in either case, but one up North was chosen; a hospital that would become well known for the expertise of its medical staff in repairing the wounds inflicted during the 'Troubles', which were soon to commence.

And so, shortly after our arrival, my mother gave birth to my sister Gudrun. By a strange coincidence, on this day years before she had given birth to her first-born, my brother Anthony. The significance of this date would not be lost on me 32 years later, when in a way, in honour of my sister, I started a new life on that same date. Gudrun was meant to signify a new beginning, the first and only one of us born in Ireland, albeit in Northern Ireland, but it was to be a false dawn.

The child had been unplanned—my parents' marriage was long past a caring loving relationship and would soon founder, and with it my unhappy sister's life would founder too.

Considering my mother's age and state of health, the birth went well enough. I recall us travelling in the sky-blue builder's van, still with its German licence plates, then our only mode of transport, to pay our first visit to the hospital to see the tiny beautiful bundle that was my sister Gudrun. Soon after my father went to collect my mother and the newborn in an oval wicker basket, which would be her bed for some time to come. It was strange to hear the cries of the new arrival echoing in the old house, which had been dormant and empty for so long and yet must have seen so many infants born there over many generations.

Anthony also came to visit us from Germany to see his new sister, having finished his first term at university. They would prove to be a few illusory rare days, when our whole family, now enlarged to six, would once more spend time under one roof. It would not last long and before Beech Mount House was finished with us, there would be only four family members left and those would be scattered. These were times of great change, and as I continued to grow and to undergo all the transformations that entailed, the whole world seemed to be going through a metamorphosis too, emerging out of an idealistic youth and facing the realities of a grown-up age.

What I clearly remember of that time is that while Anthony was there on his first visit, we watched the news with growing dismay as the short-lived Prague Spring was crushed remorselessly with the deployment of Soviet troops and tanks in the streets. Anthony and I were very upset, shedding tears with helpless frustration and out of a sense of solidarity with those who had bravely dared to challenge their oppressors. I even contemplated getting to Prague somehow to join in anti-Soviet demonstrations. The image of a student waving the Czechoslovak tri-colour in front of an advancing tank is still burnt into my memory. Alexander Dubcek was overthrown, but it would not be much longer before the Soviet adventure would implode.

That was the world at large as my mother returned to Beech Mount quite exhausted after the birth. It took all her energy to look after the baby in her ill-equipped surroundings, but she did her best to give Gudrun the attention she needed while still carrying on with most of the housework and cooking. We did not get into town that much as the first few months were filled with heavy toil from morning into the evening, with my father always an unsatisfied taskmaster. The task in question was to transform a three-storey semi-derelict house into something fit again for human habitation; not only for us, but also to create suitable accommodation fit for the first paying guests, as soon as possible. This would be essential to sustain our living costs and cover the running expenses of the house itself.

It was in this early period in Ireland when another important incident took place, for me another significant milestone, which is embedded in my memory and has remained as vivid as if it happened yesterday.

As we had no power tools I was given the job of creating an opening through the two-foot thick outside wall to accommodate a new toilet waste pipe on the third floor of the house. As the pipe was at floor level, this required crouching on the floor and using a heavy hammer and stone chisel to find the fissures in the irregular stone work. I had to chip away at the limestone blocks while avoiding the hammer bouncing off it, and dust or splinters injuring unprotected eyes. It was literally blistering work and I remember taking a break, talking to my mother down in the yard.

Next thing I heard my father shouting from upstairs for me to get back up there and get on with the job. I made some retort to the effect that I was only taking a short, well deserved break, which was enough to make him lose his temper. He screamed down for me to come up at once, or maybe it was time that he disciplined me like he did when I was only a child.

His reference to disciplining me like a child roused me into a final act of defiance. I shouted back upstairs that he knew where I was and I was ready and waiting. My mother looked on aghast and my heart was pounding, but there was silence and my father never came. I had asserted myself. I had called his bluff and he never again raised a hand against me. Ironically, while I was going through such gender confusion in my head, this was probably the first time my father had seen me as a man.

These incidents are significant markers in my relation-ship with my father and go a long way to explain the lack of warmth and compassion between us. He was never able to show me love; he always demanded respect, but that he never achieved either, because real respect must be earned not through fear, but through positive deeds and guidance.

Having in a way set myself free from my father's bonds, I now wanted to get back to work anywhere but at home. With my insistence, we started looking at positions within travel agencies for which I had, after all, trained for nearly three years.

There were at that time only about four small companies dealing with travel and tours taking in the two nearest provincial towns. These were family run businesses with a couple of girls employed for general duties. In general there were almost only girls employed in such ventures at that time and however I felt inside, there was no opportunity whatsoever to get a job within the industry I had chosen. My two and a half years of low-wage training had been wasted.

It was by now in everyone's interest to find me work. After all, I could then make a financial contribution, however small, to the tight family budget. For me it would mean a little money of my own, a greater sense of independence, and I would get away from the strained atmosphere at home.

At this time my father was engaging in another joint venture with a local businessman, trying to set up a plastics extrusion operation. At times, he would take his lunch at the local hotel, and there asked the hotel owners if they might have a job opportunity for me.

The work was initially not much more than taking drink orders, collecting glasses, general cleaning and so on. This job was not to last more than a few weeks, but it was to become the industry I would work in, with only short interludes, for more or less the next decade.

I can still remember the first night working there during a late evening function. The place was packed and I was thrown in at the deep end. My English was very rudimentary and I had great difficulty understanding the drink orders I was collecting at the tables. There were quite a few mistakes and mishaps, but to their credit the punters were very forgiving and I made a lot of tips in spite of my shortcomings. There were not many foreigners working in Ireland at that time and I suppose the guests found my accent cute, and everyone wanted to hear my story.

The novelty of working there, however, soon wore off and I was conscious that I was working in a low-wage job without proper training or a career path, at the whim of the employer who could always find someone to take my place. When I wasn't working in the hotel I was working at Beech Mount House, our home, if you could call it that, as it was still anything but comfortable or homely. It wasn't more than a few weeks later that I got the sack for giving 'back-cheek', as it was called.

***

Throughout this period my inner feelings remained, as always, hidden and suppressed, but occasionally a situation would arise where I might find some time alone in the house and indulge myself with dressing up in my mother's clothes once more. I would go so far as wearing complete outfits, even though I would have wished for more up-to-date fashions than those my mother's wardrobe had to offer. I also experimented with make-up, and my skills slowly improved. But these were always fraught moments, filled with excitement but also danger and anxiety, as I was never quite sure who might call unexpectedly, or if my parents might return early.

If these actual opportunities were rare, there were other ways to compensate and to confuse myself. As with any normal teenager of this age, I had a healthy sex drive, which could of course, given the circumstances, only be satisfied by masturbation. Except where 'normal' boys might have fantasised about a dream girl, once again I would have fantasised about being a dream girl. I was as confused as ever.

\*\*\*

The chronology of events is a little hazy after all these years, but I think it was shortly afterwards that my father got a job of assisting with the erecting of a grain silo in a market town in the neighbouring county.

For the next few weeks I worked with my father on erecting the high frame for this silo. At least he worked at the lower levels welding some very untidy looking seams, while I assisted higher up holding iron bars in place. I remember my father looking a little faint at times while I balanced on narrow steel trusses higher up. Amazingly this structure still stands.

Fellow workers used to send me to the local shop to get a 'glass hammer' and other items, often ruder, knowing that I didn't have a clue what I was asking for. I was oblivious and they were amused. It was fine. At lunchtime I could eat my sandwiches and use the few minutes to use my fishing rod to tempt the small brown trout in the river running right behind the building site.

When this contract was finished I had to look for work again. Having now worked in one hotel and having persuaded the owners to give me some sort of reference I now had to look at other hotels in the surrounding area and present myself for interview. There really were not many local options and it was in a hotel in a busy village astride the main Dublin road, where I next found employment in September 1968.

The owner, a thrifty Tyrone man, offered me a position as barman. Again the position was in line with the low wages generally paid in this industry at the time. Outside Dublin the hotel and catering industry was not unionised, there was a ready supply of unskilled labour, and you could take it or leave it. As I wanted to earn and be independent, I took it.

With no transport and bad cross country links, I now had no option but to take this job on a live-in basis and so, within months of arriving in this new country, I was living alone for the first time, even though my parents had refused me the chance to stay and continue my life and work in Germany only months earlier because I was too young.

This hotel relied on functions, dinner dances and weddings. There certainly were nice settings for wedding photos in the spacious gardens by the riverside as well as the regular restaurant and bar trade. Initially, I got on well with everyone.

\*\*\*

Whenever I had a weekend off I would do what most teenagers aspired to do in Ireland at that time; go to one of the popular large ballrooms and listen to a big band. Despite what my dreams of being a girl might lead you to believe, like every other teenage boy, I had raging hormones, and was curious about 'courting'.

I was quite amazed by this Irish dancing scene, as it was so unlike the entertainment teenagers in Germany would engage in. Usually the ballrooms would only fill up when the bars had closed and though the ballrooms were alcohol-free many of the dancers would arrive well oiled. It was rare that a dance night would pass without some skirmish; sometimes it seemed more like full-blown mayhem. The bouncers would then dive in and eventually order would be restored, though at times the local Gardaí had to make an appearance to bring matters to a conclusion.

That was one aspect I had not witnessed previously, but more peculiar to me was the very way the dances usually progressed. Anybody not in a couple usually found themselves on one side of the ballroom, divided along gender lines. When the call of, 'Next dance, please,' came from the band, there would be a general stampede across the dance floor, milling with the dancers just disentangling themselves from their last dance partners to grab the hand of the girl you wanted to dance with next.

It was quite comical to watch, but also very intimidating, because I was shy and it took me a lot of time before I could muster the courage and the necessary speed to get to the desired dance partner and not to be left empty-handed and embarrassed.

Normally there would be a couple of quicksteps, where jiving was the thing to do and many could do it very well. That would be followed by a slow dance. The guys might use a quick dance to check out the girl they fancied and if they got any kind of positive reaction or encouragement, they would try to get in there again to follow up with a slow dance and get into closer contact. Having been to dance school in Germany wasn't a real advantage here, because for any slow dance the floor would soon be crowded and basically everyone shuffled in a clockwise fashion around the floor, trying to make the usual, 'Do you come here often?' small talk.

Looking back at it now so many years later, it all seems to have had an air of innocence about it and I think at times I just enjoyed standing back and watching the whole predictable ritual as much as actually getting involved in it.

The objective would be to have someone to leave with, to bring home, and by the time last dance was called you could see desperation in many eyes as they threw caution to the wind to succeed with the last dance. Then, the national anthem would be sung at the end of the night. Everyone stood, if able, usually singing along, which was another curious thing for me, as singing the national anthem at the end of every public function was certainly new. In Germany, that belonged to another, darker era.

More rows would often ensue as the dances finished—rows over girls, rows over jumping the queue at the chippy, rows just for the sake of rows as so often the influence of drink seriously impairs all common sense. There would be young couples with happy radiant faces, cuddling and kissing. There would be others getting sick with drink, singing and swearing, a picturesque noisy melee, which could be found around this time on a Saturday night in any Irish town with a ballroom.

My first liaisons were formed here. First there was a short encounter lasting maybe no more than a few weekends with a young neighbour's daughter, but then I started going out with a nice girl of whom I grew very fond. Jane was very attractive, with long chestnut brown hair and matching brown eyes. She was obviously from a good home as she never cursed and she was very well mannered.

Our relationship never went beyond anything more serious than kissing and petting. In due course I also met her parents, who were quite old already as Jane was the youngest in her family. Her father had a smallholding, a few cattle, and also worked in the local factory. They were also very polite, but I don't believe they ever really warmed to me. After all, I was a foreigner with a bit of an accent, and Protestant to boot, which to most Catholic families would not have been particularly good news at that time. Whether it was her parents' disapproval or not, Jane ended our relationship after about six months and I was heartbroken for a while.

There were some others—one night stands you might say, though today that would conjure up a meaning I do not intend, as I really was still very innocent then. Today any 18 or 19-year-old would not readily admit to not having had sex, but it was a different age then, and not worse for that.

Angela was another girl that I met in the ballroom and dated for a short while. She was small, elfin-like with big eyes and very long, wavy hair. When my elder brother Anthony later came to live in Ireland I pointed her out to him one night as one of my previous girlfriends. He promptly asked her to dance and there followed a long relationship lasting some six years. They lived first in Ireland and later in England together. As far as I know she moved to the West of Ireland and, last I heard, lives a very alternative, close-to-nature lifestyle.

About a year after my arrival in Ireland, I used the little 50cc motor-bike I had acquired on hire purchase for a first return trip to Germany, even unwittingly using the UK motorways illegally and riding through atrocious weather before reaching the continent more than a little saddle sore.

There, in a fashionable little boutique, I spied a waist-length tight fitting leather jacket with a diagonal zip, and though it was clear that this was a women's boutique or maybe because of it, I had to have that jacket, and I bought it.

This would almost become my trademark—when you saw someone approaching on a little motorbike, wearing a blue and white helmet and a leather jacket, well, that just had to be me. I loved that jacket dearly, because in Ireland fashion was dreary, especially what boys wore, and it made me stand out. But I also knew that this was a girl's leather jacket and it made it all the more right for me.

I eventually arrived in Germany and I stayed at my granny's flat. From there I visited my few friends and former colleagues and though of course everyone was intrigued at my journey and wanted to know all about living in Ireland, the novelty soon wore off and they naturally returned to their personal topics and gossip, which I was no longer part of. In that one short year, I had not yet truly integrated myself totally with life in Ireland, but I also no longer belonged here in my former surroundings. Not belonging quite here nor there is a condition which seems to define my life!

# CHAPTER 7

## KAREN

Having been sacked from the hotel meant that I needed to find another job and I did so almost immediately at a pub in the neighbouring village.

Now I would be employed as barman at the Inn, which at that time was made up of a restaurant, the public bar and adjoining lounge, a little grocery shop and petrol pumps. Today there is still an Inn, but the place has been redeveloped and changed ownership a couple of times so it is hardly recognisable from the place I went to work in back then.

The owners then, my now new employers, were two partners, though I would be dealing mostly with the landlord living upstairs above the pub with his wife and five children. Liam was a genial publican and a fair employer. I now worked for the princely sum of £10 per week, but I also had to find some low cost accommodation somewhere, because this was no longer a live-in position. With Liam's large family there was no room at the inn, so to speak.

I heard about a lady nearby, whose husband had died recently, leaving her now living alone.

More out of interest in some company than commercial necessity, Mrs O'Brien was willing to let some of the furnished rooms in her house to young single people, who were in need of simple and inexpensive accommodation. I took one of the rooms upstairs. Mrs O'Brien was a nice old lady, and though she did appear a little stern at times, she really had her heart in the right place.

The Inn was known as a singing pub. There would usually be entertainment on most weekend nights and in the summer there could be additional nights during the week. Musical entertainment would take place in the lounge which had seating for maybe 40 people, though it would often be crowded with far more than that. The lounge had quite a low ceiling, the air conditioning was usually quite useless, the air often thick with smoke and very hard on sensitive eyes. The acoustics, due to the L-shaped layout of the place, were also poor. Many a good night was had there and it was never easy to get everyone out at closing time.

It was on such a night when I first set eyes on Karen. It would probably be right to say that this was the most significant meeting in my life, though of course I could not know that at the time. Karen would be a part of my life for the next three decades, bear our three children and share the joys and sorrows of everyday life as well as many adventures with me. Though we parted from our joint path, we have remained and hopefully will always remain friends.

That evening a family singing group was due to play. I had not heard of them before and as far as I was concerned it would be just another busy night, but as they came in to set up their equipment, I noticed that one member of that group was an attractive girl. She was slim with a face framed by long straight light-brown hair, cut simply with a fringe. She was wearing a mini-dress with narrow blue and white stripes, which she had customised a little to make it more interesting. The dress was accentuating her nice long legs.

She didn't smile much as she stood on the tight stage. If anything she looked rather bored in a sort of 'here we go again' kind of way. Though on their promotional photo she was displayed playing a guitar, she did in fact accompany the mostly country and western music with a large tambourine. But when it was her turn to sing, she would become more animated. Mostly she sang pop tunes of the day, as well as country and western classics. There is no doubt that I fell in love with her voice immediately; she had me in her spell. Whenever I could I would steal a glance across the bar in her direction and when she saw me she returned my smile, and I found it hard to concentrate on my work for the rest of the night. Being with the band, very nicely dressed and wearing a little make-up, it was impossible to believe that she was then only 14 years old.

At the end of the night I managed to get her to sit with me at the bar for a few minutes to make conversation, no doubt watched carefully by her parents. Her father, Bobby, was a good singer. A Jim Reeves fan, he also played the drums and did most of the talking. Having been self-trained on the drums, his talking was certainly better than his drum playing in those days.

Karen's mother Caroline carried most of the melody of the music with her 'electrovox', a sort of electric accordion, which could make a variety of sounds. She could play that instrument well, but it wasn't necessarily the kind of music I would have been inclined to listen to if it hadn't been for Karen's singing. The last member of the group was Karen's brother Richard on the lead guitar.

While I can still recall the scene, the looks, even the atmosphere, I can no longer recall what exactly we talked about in those few minutes at the bar, but of course I complimented Karen on her beautiful singing and I am sure I made it pretty obvious that I was smitten, as they say. It must have made some impression, because it would launch the most important relationship of my life.

Karen gave me a little background and I learned that they lived quite close by in a local village, just a few miles up the road from my digs. She gave me one of their promotional band photos and she told me where they would be playing over the next few days. I promised that I would come along to listen to them on my first available free night.

That first time I went to listen to Karen and her family ensemble was in a loud and rough working man's pub in a nearby town, but loud and rough could have been the description for many of the singing pubs then, something I would get more or less used to over the years. The men drank their pints, the women could hold their own with them, they would sing their songs and quite often there might be a row thrown in for extra entertainment. Anyway, if I wanted to see Karen, this was then the only way, because her parents wouldn't have allowed anything else.

On that first night I arrived in my new leather jacket, under which I wore a light blue velvety jumper and bell-bottom trousers. I stood out from the crowd alright! You could see people gawping, including Karen's very suspicious mother, who enquired of her: 'What is that fellow doing here?'

This first meeting after our initial encounter was nerve-wracking. I could be very extroverted in terms of clothes and appearance, but at the same time I was quite shy when it came to such situations. The only time I could actually get to talk to Karen was during their mid-session break and a few minutes after they finished, and while her father and brother packed up their gear. We talked a little more about who we were and Karen said the next time I should just come to their house just before they would be due to leave and I could then get a lift with them to and from the venue.

This more or less became a sort of routine thereafter. On any night I did not have to work and they were playing at some venue, I would walk the mile from my digs along the twisty road to hover around their house, waiting for them to load up and appear at the last minute and ask if I could come along. Karen would then tell me afterwards about having to face the inquisition—they wanted to know all about me—and while they were quite cordial to me, they did try to get Karen to stop seeing me.

However, we did see each other as much as possible and it wasn't long before we arranged to meet for a walk, where we would not be supervised. Somewhere the first kisses were exchanged and before long we were 'going together'.

Karen's parents had met some 16 years earlier and married soon after. Karen's birth was followed by a succession of siblings in the following years.

I found all of this out when I met and fell in love with Karen in that Indian summer. For me there was nothing conflicting about this romance, because it was natural for me as a young man to find romance with a young woman, and my private desires—my dreams and my experimenting with women's clothes and make-up—just didn't come into the equation to the extent that I gave them any thought. I didn't want to mention anything about it to Karen, for obvious reasons. And anyway, I was a young man, and Karen was a young woman; our being together just seemed like the most natural thing in the world. Why would I want to change that?

# CHAPTER 8

## MICHAEL

As I mentioned earlier, the Inn where I now worked and first met Karen, was owned by two partners. As well as Liam who lived with his family above the pub, there was Michael. This man played a hugely significant part in my life and made me realise some very important things on my journey of self-discovery.

One of Michael's relatives was a Fenian Patriot, who had lived among and been close to people within the Irish Republican Brotherhood and the founders of the Gaelic League. Michael also liked to refer to himself as a 'Fenian bastard'. He was a middle-aged single man living alone in a rented cottage up a quiet lane about a mile from the pub. His love of history, albeit strongly flavoured by his republicanism, made him appealing to me, as I have always loved history.

As a newcomer to Ireland I took a keen interest in politics. I knew I would have to understand Ireland's history to understand its people. So we had something in common and soon we would debate the right and wrongs of Irish history and politics at large while restocking the shelves after a busy night.

At this time politics was entering a new and dangerous phase; the civil rights movement in Ireland was not so much running out of steam as being battered to the ground by intransigent rulers and this was leading to what would prove a long and tortuous cycle of violence.

Michael would recall for me all the wrongs of British politics in Ireland, read some of his grandfather's poetry or rant at the latest news from Northern Ireland. There always seemed to be an air of sadness in him, a frustration of a life unfulfilled.

Michael spent little time in the pub and then only to help occasionally with things like restocking shelves, and maybe looking over the accounts. Whatever way their business partnership had come about, Liam was not that keen to have Michael actually serving the clients. Not surprisingly, because he was clumsy and usually grumpy and gruff with customers. They in turn did not like him.

It seemed as if Michael had a disdain for the simple needs and intellect of the average county folk frequenting the pub during the day. Yet we built a good rapport based on our shared interests. In a way it was strange, because here I was, just about 19, a Protestant German, brought up in a city, and there was Michael, a middle-aged Catholic from small town Ireland.

It took a little while for me to realise that there was more to Michael's often awkward and abrupt manner with others, and the reason why most of the locals didn't engage with him. Michael was gay, which in Ireland, especially rural Ireland, meant being treated like an outcast, to be the subject of hurtful remarks, the butt of jokes, whispers behind raised hands and sideward glances.

For anyone growing up in Ireland, having the misfortune of being gay was, until recently, anything but easy. It drove many good and worthy people into isolation, into sordid situations for want of any other outlets for their sexuality, or to despair and even suicide.

For me it was also a little disconcerting, because I had not really encountered any gay men before, and far more confusing was the fact that it became more and more obvious that Michael was developing feelings for me. Added to this was my own obvious confusion; I was still dressing up whenever I could, but was as interested in women as any young man was. I didn't understand these conflicting feelings, and didn't exactly have a world of information to turn to in order to find answers.

This all led in the end to an unfortunate incident, which I have never shared with anyone and which I later very much regretted. Had I made it quite clear from the start that I enjoyed Michael's friendship in an intellectual way, but it could never mean more than that, I think he would have accepted that and we would have continued as before.

If I did not give those signals in a clear and unequivocal way, that is partly due to the fact that I did not want to hurt him, because I felt sorry for his predicament and isolation. He did know that I was now seeing a girl, namely Karen, whom after all I had met right there in the pub, where we would usually have our debates. In a way, he never acknowledged that and maybe he hoped that in spite of it I might be otherwise inclined.

No doubt it must have been difficult for Michael to take a risk and tell me about his sexuality. After all, I could have rejected him in the way he was used to from most people he met. Because he had been so open with me, I told him a little about my own gender identity confusions—not that I would have used such terminology then, as it was totally alien to me. I just mentioned the fact that I secretly dressed in female clothing occasionally, and just saying that out loud to someone, making it real, gave me a great sense of tranquillity. Maybe Michael misread the signals originating from my gender confusion, as is so easily done.

One day we talked about books and poetry and Michael told me about some books I would be welcome to borrow. He suggested I come out sometime to his cottage for that purpose, but the way he looked at me made it obvious, even to someone as inexperienced as me, that this was about more than books. This should have been the moment when I made an excuse, spoken in a way that could only have been interpreted as a rejection of his invitation, though couched in magnanimous language. Instead I said I would come up one evening to have a look around his cottage.

My going along with this didn't come about because of anything that Michael did or didn't do. After all, Michael just wanted a young man he was falling in love with to fall in love with him too. I, on the other hand, acted not out of love or even any kind of physical attraction for Michael, but for selfish motives. Michael would be a means for me to be treated as the girl I secretly longed to be.

One dark autumn evening I rode my bike the short distance up the quiet lane to Michael's cottage. Happily, there was nobody about who might have noticed me turning off the road or witnessed me either entering or later leaving the cottage.

Michael greeted me warmly and I could see the welling emotion in his eyes. The place looked untidy and cluttered; a typical middle-aged bachelor's place. There isn't much I can remember about the exact sequence of events, or maybe my mind has blocked them out, because they are too painful. Somewhere along the way Michael kissed me and I did not resist. He fumbled awkwardly and half undressed me down to the female underwear I was wearing. Quickly, I was in an aroused trance with my eyes closed, pretending hard to have that girl's body I craved for, imagining being loved by a handsome young guy, not the middle-aged homosexual who was in fact there with me. My warm wasted seed soon blew away any pretensions of being the perfect-bodied girl. I had orgasmed, but only because I had felt his touch as if I were a woman, the sensation of which was too much for my young body, which responded purely to the physical stimulation, and nothing more.

I looked down in disgust at myself with tears welling up and Michael stood there half-naked, his quickly diminishing member in his hand, and he didn't quite know what to do as I dressed hurriedly, mumbled some apologies, and fled the scene.

Our next meeting in the pub was obviously difficult, but we never discussed this sad episode in any detailed way. There was never a repeat performance and Michael accepted that whatever I was, it did not seem to be a fellow homosexual. I think he appreciated that I at least was willing to continue our old platonic friendship.

We met from time to time even long after I had left the Inn. Mostly Karen would be with me, but Michael had little time for young girls, especially one who had taken the boy he liked. Karen knew nothing of what had happened, as she knew nothing of my cross-dressing, and accepted his occasional visits as if he were just another friend, because we could talk politics or history, neither of which interested her.

I dealt with what had happened mostly by burying it, because I could not understand the implications. I thought to myself: well, at least you're not homosexual, but with hindsight I feel that I misled Michael with my lack of clarity and burdened him with a hopeless, one-sided unrequited love. I thought this revelation would clarify things for me, but if anything it just made me more confused. I knew for sure that I was not gay, but I then had to come to terms with the fact that I had no idea what, or who, I was. All I knew was that I wanted to be treated, touched and loved as a woman, which of course could not happen because I was quite clearly a man, and one with the usual male sexual drives to boot.

\*\*\*

Michael was very proud later on when I asked him to become my godfather, though he was not particularly enamoured of any church that would condemn him for his sexuality. He later also stayed with us after I got married and we spent a memorable day pony-trekking.

Some years later, Michael had a heart attack and was convalescing for some time in hospital, where I visited him once or twice. He was chiding me gently for not seeing him more often. When we had moved to London, Michael had a second heart attack and died. I went to his funeral, which was well attended, considering that there was really no surviving close family. In life he had been largely shunned, but the Irish love a funeral and mostly don't see the hypocrisy. Michael is buried in a quiet country graveyard.

Michael was a man who would have been most happy to have been born either a century earlier, sharing the romantic patriotism of the Irish Republican Brotherhood, or alternatively half a century later, when his sexuality would no longer have been important enough to mar his whole life. I hope he rests in poetic peace, where human intolerance can no longer cause any pain.

# CHAPTER 9

## 1970

At the end of the 1960s it was time to take stock. My life had been turned upside down over the past couple of years. My certainties, if ever there were any, had been taken away one by one. Germany and my old life were history. My apprenticeship had been left unfinished, my old home and friends were just memories and the promised new home never came to be, as I was now already living alone in my modest rented room. On top of that, despite my relationship with Karen, I was still experiencing confusing feelings about my gender, which I tried not to think about too much. I tried to keep it a secret from everyone, so it was better to put it to the back of my mind too.

On almost every level I seemed to struggle to fit in. What I had was not a career but just a series of jobs without any real prospects of either advancement or material prosperity. Indeed it was a real struggle to even have a very limited social life on what I was earning and there was a terrible spell of unemployment as well.

As for my erstwhile ideals of somehow participating in making the world a better place, they were never very realistic to begin with, but now, cut off in rural Ireland, those ideals looked very far fetched indeed.

On a personal level I did not even know who I really was or was meant to be. Whenever these questions arose in my consciousness, I would find ways to either rationalise them away or to suppress them altogether. Because it was easy in these years of the late 1960s and early 1970s to dress in quite an androgynous fashion, I didn't have to face up to any malingering doubts in my mind and, after all, had I not fallen in love with a nice girl? And had my one would-be homosexual encounter not been an utter failure? Therefore, I reasoned, my secret female desires would fade in time and I could just become that normal regular guy, if only I gave myself time.

Nowadays there are more counsellors than you can shake a stick at, and of course, all you need to do is type a few words into your computer and the world-wide-web is at your fingertips. But this was still a different age; sex education was done in whispers with dire warnings of the consequences of illicit sex—unwanted pregnancy—but little else. Anyone with anything that might be considered out of the ordinary held their own counsel.

So I did. Instead of seeking help, I tried to live with myself as best I could. I started reading a lot, usually my favourite novels with some historical background, to divert my thoughts and at the same time maybe to find some answers to my questions, like: what is the meaning of it all and where is God among the mayhem?

Looking back at some of my poetry of the time, it is evident that I was a tortured soul, agonising over all the injustices in the world.

For some reason I started writing a diary for one year with entries dating from 17 May 1970 to 16 May 1971. It was in many ways an extremely eventful period in my life on every level and while I was trying to make sense of what was happening, I wrote about everything, not just what was going on inside my head. I felt unable to communicate my feelings, not only of confusion, but frustration, and sometimes joy, with others.

The often melodramatic has to be seen in its context. I was genuinely wrestling to make sense of my world; the world at large, which at that time was dominated by regular news of atrocities; and my personal world, which was threatening to fall apart.

In many ways I was living a lie. Much of what I wrote then looks quite naïve now looking back more than three decades later, but then things often appear different with the wisdom, or maybe cynicism, of hindsight.

What is most striking, for me, is the fact that all of these things that I would speak about in my diary would be so typical of a normal young man and his preoccupations. Family troubles, oversensitivity, sex, independence, new ideologies and the questioning of old ones—all are dealt with in these diaries the way they would be by any young man.

But what is also noticeable is that there is no mention of my secret desires; as if I dared not even mention them to myself for fear of making them real through expressing them on paper. They were ever-present in this time—of that there is no doubt—but I dared not let myself believe it. The diary starts with the following foreword written by me 34 years ago ...

\*\*\*

*'There is no special reason why this diary should start on 17 May. On this day I felt like putting my thoughts to paper. It is accidental that it starts with a few depressing thoughts. This diary is part of my soul. It will show the ups and downs of human life.*

*By the time I re-read things I wrote months (or years) before, I might think different; I might have changed by then, because we are all subject to changes on which not we, but the people around us often have great influence.*

*Maybe it is the hope that we and with us society will change for the better, which keeps us going.*

*So do not be astonished, dear reader, whoever you are, when reading this diary you will find things familiar to you, because whether you are black or white, Catholic or Jew, we are all the same God-made men.'*

\*\*\*

Perhaps I was desperate to hold on to Karen, and blind to what was going on, because losing her might mean that my validation as an ordinary man would be gone too, and I would no longer be able to dismiss my other side.

Then, amidst the very volatile political situation in the North, the event that finally scattered our last vestiges of family life occurred. My parents separated.

My father was soon gone from Beech Mount. He returned at least temporarily to Germany leaving my mother to look after the family. The separation must have been terrible for my poor mother, who had been married for more than 20 years and now faced looking after us and the house alone.

That summer I had also taken my little bike for a second trip to Germany, but then as I was speeding to see Karen on the date of our first anniversary, I crashed my bike almost head-on into an oncoming car. My bike was a write-off and I ended up miraculously with no broken bones, though on crutches for some weeks to come.

Then in the autumn a major fire at Beech Mount House completely destroyed the recently converted and refurbished horse stable building, leading to a ten year battle with insurers for compensation, due to the fact that arson was the cause. The fire much reduced the available guest accommodation and with it my mother's future potential income.

\*\*\*

Two incidents which left their indelible mark on me also happened at this time in the run-up to Christmas 1970. One of these events I have spent a lifetime regretting, while the other changed my life profoundly, though very gradually.

As usual I was broke—my very low wages made it really difficult to save up for any special occasions—but Christmas was coming and everyone was talking about buying presents for family and friends.

I couldn't see how my meagre £16 savings was going to buy worthwhile presents for Karen and also some bits and pieces for other family members. I went to Dublin to look for some interesting bargains, but just about everything seemed to be out of my reach. I had visions of being totally embarrassed on Christmas Day, receiving presents and not being able to give anything adequate in return.

Liam, my erstwhile employer at the Inn had given me a horse racing tip for my birthday. I still remember the name of the horse: Razor's Edge. I had never previously backed a horse, but I ventured a £1 bet and the horse won at 8/1. £8 now seems like nothing, but to me at that time it was almost an extra week's wages.

It would have been better though, if that horse had lost, because I could have managed with a pound less and would have learned immediately that generally only the bookies win in horse racing.

I decided to put all my money on another hotly-tipped horse. Cautiously, or so I thought at the time, I made it an each-way bet. My horse came nowhere in the race and I was crestfallen. I ran out of the bookies in a right state. If things had looked bad before, now they were infinitely worse. Instead of inadequate presents, there would be no presents at all.

I desperately tried to figure out a way to get the money back. There seemed to be nobody I could turn to; I had no accounts, no credit rating and there would be no options of loans. And so, after considerable internal wrestling, self-justification and wayward reasoning, I decided to steal the money.

Writing about this is still painful, even after all these years. It is the one moment of my life I am truly ashamed of and I never quite managed to forgive myself. I went into a hardware shop and bought a small kitchen knife with the few shillings I had left.

I wandered around the quieter streets of North Dublin and walked into a small neighbourhood grocery shop in an agitated state. The store was empty, except for a middle-aged lady, very likely the proprietor. I demanded money with the knife in my hand. She opened the till and stood aside, and I took exactly £16. She must have thought I was a very odd thief not to take the lot when I had the chance.

If she had refused I would have run empty-handed—there never was any intent of using the kitchen knife, but then the woman didn't know that and I have endlessly regretted putting her through that frightening ordeal, even though it barely lasted more than a few seconds.

Once I left the shop I ran back into busier streets with my heart pounding, feeling as though everyone was looking at me in an accusing sort of way and there would be a tap on my shoulder at any moment and I would be taken away in disgrace.

When some time had passed and I had calmed down I bought some small presents—those I had rejected earlier as inadequate. If the recipients were disappointed, they didn't show it, but if they had known what those presents cost me in years of regret later, or what they had cost the woman in the grocery store, they would have been horrified.

This episode taught me a lot; for one thing it stopped me gambling before I ever got started. It also taught me progressively to hate the commercialism of Christmas, which encourages us to compete with each other for presents, irrespective of our ability to afford them. It taught me that the best presents are free and to be less prejudicial of others who have offended in similar ways.

The small sum of money never was worth the gnawing sense of guilt I felt for a long time after. I often considered repaying the debt to the shopkeeper in person, but I was frightened that I would end up in trouble with the police.

When I had a similar sum to spare sometime later, I made an anonymous donation of exactly £16 during a church collection.

The other much more positive event, which had a profound effect on my life and also in due course let me come to terms with my sense of guilt and shame over the earlier incident, was a chance encounter with a highly respected Monsignor.

One day I was hitching a lift. After a long wait a large dark blue Mercedes pulled up. The driver, who was an elderly man wore a dog-collar, not the standard priest's dog-collar, but one with added purple to designate him as a Monsignor, though I did not know that until he introduced himself to me.

On the slow journey we were soon engaged in deep conversation. I had twice tried to approach a Catholic priest but had backed off due to nervousness, but this man seemed kind and wise, and I took his address and the kind invitation to come and talk to him whenever I wanted.

This would prove to be one of the defining meetings of my life, because it helped me to challenge my own beliefs and to accept my faith.

By then the Monsignor was already over 80 years old and serving as the Parish Priest in a quiet parish, where he could see out the end of his priestly vocation.

It transpired that the Monsignor was a Doctor of both Theology and Philosophy and had also studied and learned German. We may even have exchanged a few words in German just for the hell of it, though that is probably the wrong expression to use in this context.

The Monsignor soon saw that I held strong opinions on politics, faith and history, and was particularly critical of the history of the Catholic Church. I also told him where I worked and a little about myself. When we arrived at our destination we both felt that our conversation had been stimulating and that we should meet again.

That Christmas I met and spoke to the Monsignor several times, and he helped me through what was a poor part of my life, both literally and spiritually, and for that I will always be grateful. I kept my inner turmoil to myself though.

# Chapter 10

## 1971 Onward

No doubt 1970 had been a difficult year for me, but at the very end there was hope for the future. There was my continuing relationship with the girl I loved, though I would never tell her about my secret inner feelings, and then, surprisingly, there was the security of newfound faith.

I can't quite remember how often I met up with the Monsignor, but soon afterwards we met at a small convent with a few mostly elderly nuns in residence. The Monsignor was warmly welcomed there and soon food and a bottle of sherry appeared. There we were, the octogenarian Irish priest and the young reluctant German Protestant.

At the same time, I was still enjoying my every meeting with Karen, and I struggled to keep my hormonal urges in check, but I prevailed, and we kept seeing each other.

I guess I was desperately holding on to the idea of Karen as my girlfriend in what were troubled times for me. I did love her, as I still do, but perhaps the added meaning that she was part of my being a normal man was what drove me on, and when I faced losing her, sometimes drove me to despair. I subconsciously feared that without her my secret desires would no longer be kept in check, and would send me spiralling into confusion.

***

It was at my behest that the Monsignor made some introductions for me and I commenced with instructions in the Catholic faith at a Friary Church where a most gentle Friar helped me on my path. It culminated in my second baptism and confirmation.

There were many people who always thought that my conversion from Protestant to Catholic was some act of convenience because I would not be able to marry a Catholic Irish girl as a Protestant foreigner, but that couldn't be further from the truth.

For me this was a spiritual journey, which intensified over the years and my faith helped me through some of the most traumatic events in my life.

I wanted to leave behind a Lutheran God, who we had been taught to be in awe of, to fear his wrath, for a God, who loves us in spite of our sins and who is merciful.

It is of course regrettable, with hindsight, that I never found the courage to discuss my inner gender related confusion with the Monsignor, but it was just too intimate, too difficult. After all he was a priest belonging to a very dogmatic and conservative church and then there was also the big age gap and I just couldn't bring myself to talk about something so personal and yet so troubling for me. At this time I really still thought this was so different, so challenging, that no one would ever understand and I would risk losing all sense of friendship and the sympathy of anyone I dared to take into my confidence.

\*\*\*

Across the border in South Armagh and in Belfast the conflict was reaching new levels of violence and depravation on all sides and many of the most wanted terrorists or freedom fighters, depending on one's political viewpoint, seemed to seek refuge in the town where I lived.

In 1972, at the very height of conflict, I decided to go hitching for a few days. I really wanted to form my own opinion about what the country and the people were like, rather than swallow what was written in the official press or in *An Phoblacht*, the mouthpiece of the Provisional IRA.

I got all the way up to the Giant's Causeway, where, strangely enough, I remember getting one lift with a man driving an old VW Beetle from my own home city in Germany, near the village of Bushmills in County Antrim, famous for its Bushmills Whiskey.

My most informative and at the same time silly episode of that holiday occurred in the Ardoyne area of North Belfast, very much a beleaguered isolated Catholic community surrounded by staunchly Protestant areas.

Before setting off on my few days hiking adventure I bought a pair of trainers. As a foreigner, albeit one very interested in politics and history, I was still oblivious to the symbolism of colours in Northern Ireland. Therefore it was quite strange and with hindsight probably quite dangerous to walk around the streets of Belfast. Here you knew very quickly whether you were in a Loyalist or a Nationalist area.

There were either countless Union Jacks or Irish Tricolours depicting allegiance, along with colourful murals on every gable wall, glorifying various organisations with grand names and despicable deeds among their credentials. You could also just let the curbstones guide you. If they were blue, white and red, you were of course in Loyalist quarters; once they changed to green, white and orange you had entered nationalist neighbourhoods.

I had chosen my runners for comfort and the low price, and nothing else. They just happened to be white with parallel red and blue strips on the sides. Nobody would have passed any remarks about my shoes in the Republic, but when I entered the Ardoyne area, it didn't take very long before a group of people approached me and I was effectively arrested, by what they called a Citizens' Defence Committee. These committees existed in most of the nationalist neighbourhoods and were really a front for the Provisional IRA.

They marched me off to the Holy Cross School and asked me a lot of questions—apart from comments relating to my shoes—none of which I can recall. The fact that I carried my German passport along with a still noticeable German accent convinced them that I was not some agent of the crown on some undercover mission. They let me go in due course, but not before insisting that I removed the two obviously offending blue and red stripes from my shoes.

To me this one personal and absurd incident always reminds me of the entrenched bigotry of both sides in the conflict in Northern Ireland.

As it was by now dark and a very dangerous area to walk around in as a lone stranger, they not only let me go, but invited me to stay right there in the school, which was at that time offering emergency shelter to many refugees who had been burned out of their homes during vicious sectarian attacks in nearby Bombay Street.

It was here I met a young girl who was a member of the female youth wing of the IRA. She was a lovely girl, full of patriotic indignant fervour, ready to help protect her community at all costs. We had a discussion about politics till late into the night and there was even a kiss at the end of it, a kiss I felt a little guilty about later as I was, after all, spoken for.

Sadly I have forgotten the girl's name, but I have often wondered what became of her, whether, like so many who started off with genuine idealism, she got sucked in deeper and deeper into the dirty turf wars of Northern Ireland. But then again she may be a happily married woman now with a grown up family, or perhaps like many others she left for greener fields elsewhere to extricate herself from the narrow-minded bigotry of Northern Ireland.

So the 70s had made its mark on me and my life seemed to take new directions. Germany was the past, I was prepared to build a career in the hotel business, I had a girl I was in love with, I had a better understanding of Irish politics and I had made a commitment to my new faith. Only the most fundamental question, 'Who am I?' had still not been answered.

# CHAPTER 11

## DOUBTS AND COMMITMENTS

After a short while working as a barman in the hotel, I approached the general manager and co-owner to discuss how I could progress my career within their hotel group. It was decided I would be given the opportunity to work as a trainee manager, which involved periods of some months in the different hotel departments, like the kitchen or the dining room. I understood that, upon successful completion of the different phases, I would be taken on as an assistant manager. Nowadays I would of course insist on a written contract, but back then I was young and naïve and it didn't occur to me.

The one advantage of working there was the opportunity to augment the meagre wages with some tips. In those days I kept on my toes; everyone seemed to be my boss. There were many split shifts, which didn't leave me with much useful time to do anything, other than catching up on sleep or contemplating the fact that I never seemed to have any money to do anything.

On a few occasions Karen visited me in my digs. Of course her parents were never aware of these encounters.

By now we were together for some time and had progressed from kissing to more intimate body contact, thankfully always able to resist the final step to engage in intercourse for fear of its possible consequences.

Our first real intimate encounter was another significant milestone, but not for the anticipated reasons. One day we drove in my old car on to a quiet little country lane. Our normal kissing and cuddling didn't seem enough anymore, clothes were partially removed, busy hands and fingers played excitedly with each other's bits and, well, orgasms occurred. So far, so good. After all I guess everyone remembers their first adventure of this nature.

While the excitement had lasted and the red mist of testosterone had descended upon me, all seemed well, but as soon as I had ejaculated aided by someone else for the first time, not just someone else, but by the girl I loved, I started crying. I felt dirty and inadequate, I hated the sight of my genitals; I was confused. Karen reassured me and once more the questions that may have been asked were suppressed. It just wasn't talked about.

I often experienced these divided feelings from then on. I knew the sexual excitement was at times ecstasy driven by a strong testosterone-fuelled sex-drive, and I did desperately want this girl whom I loved dearly, yet I was often left with a feeling that something was amiss. Over the years I learned and refined the art of coming like a man whilst at the same time dreaming of being a submissive woman at the receiving end.

\*\*\*

It is difficult to explain the complicated workings of any brain, much less the even more complex signals of a transsexual (TS) brain. The experts are still debating it, though there is acceptance among many, based on a small number of dissected TS brains, that the brain of a male to female transsexual is essentially that of a female in relation to sexual signals. But those brain signals still have to compete with the powerful stimulus of testosterone, produced by the otherwise male anatomy.

Essentially it means that while my brain was acting like that of a woman, my body was acting very much like that of a man. I was physically attracted to women, especially Karen, but in my mind I wanted to be loved like a woman. It took me years to deal with it. This was 1972; a different age in awareness of such matters, and I just muddled through as best I could, while keeping my secret well concealed from Karen.

\*\*\*

As the time approached when I should have been promoted from trainee manager to assistant manager nothing was happening and when I asked for meetings I was constantly fobbed off.

So I used my initiative and started getting some contact addresses on the continent, the place to train if hotel management was the objective. It wasn't long before I managed to get a six-month training contract as administration trainee in a top grade hotel in a European capital city. In addition, I also managed to get six-month contracts for my two best friends in the hotel.

The contract was to run from November to April. On one hand I was really looking forward to a new challenge which would also progress my career with a proper certificate at the end of it, but on the other hand I was dreading being parted from Karen.

We decided to get engaged beforehand to show our commitment to each other and to make it easier to get through the time apart. Karen and I managed to get to Dublin and, without telling anyone, we bought an engagement ring at a jeweller's right in the heart of Dublin, on the corner of Henry Street and O'Connell Street.

This would later prove to be the first of three engagement rings, the others being lost along the way. We invited a few friends and some family members to Beech Mount and had an engagement party, though we never made any big formal announcement. It was like an engagement with subterfuge. We kept it low-key in order to avoid resistance from our parents; after all, though I was now nearly 20, Karen was still only 17.

While we were celebrating our engagement, and so making a first formal commitment to each other, that same year my parents' divorce finally came through. It was hardly surprising after all that had happened since my father's departure. My parents had lived separately since then, with my father spending time in Germany, where he met his second wife to be, the mother of my three half-sisters. My contact with my father was non-existent really at that time and I saw my mother and my baby sister only occasionally.

At a dinner dance Karen and I attended I had pictures taken and framed and they would sit by my bedside in the hotel for the next six months. I took a lock of Karen's hair and a few other personal belongings to keep her fresh in my memory.

The three of us set off that October and arrived without too much incident at the hotel in Europe. The facilities there were excellent, and modern too. Staff lived in twin rooms. My friends took one room, as they would find it easier to stay together with their lack of German, and I took up residence with a pleasant young Hungarian by the name of Arpad. He had left Hungary at a time when this was not easy to do and it would be even harder to return, and he was often a little sad and homesick. He was determined to make his fortune and someday to return to his homeland. I wouldn't be surprised if he fulfilled his dream and returned to Hungary when communism finally collapsed across Eastern Europe.

The next day we reported to the hotel and were introduced to our respective supervisors. Though I initially worked for a little while together with one of my friends, which in practice meant helping with the constant flow of major functions going on, we later did not see that much of each other at work, but we all settled into our respective routines. There wasn't too much of a language barrier for the two boys as most Europeans in the hotel industry are capable linguists and speak English as well.

Later, when I had been moved to work in the hotel's stores and supplies office, I had discovered the only direct phone line not going through the switchboard. In the evenings, I managed to sneak behind the counter to keep in touch with Karen with long and loving, and of course illicit phone calls. A couple of times I was nearly caught by the night watchman on his rounds and had to whisper to Karen to keep quiet, while I sat motionless under the counter with my heart pounding, but as it were I was never caught red-handed. Admittedly I must have run up quite a phone bill in my time there, but it was all in the name of love. Otherwise, I was as always a most conscientious worker and my superiors were always pleased with my endeavours. These conversations kept me going, particularly as Karen was not great at writing letters.

The six months went by rapidly and before our time was up I started writing to hotels in Ireland to have a decent position to return to. Once more I was successful and was offered a job as an Assistant Manager. I was ready to come home again and couldn't wait to return to Karen's arms.

\*\*\*

It wasn't long after the heartfelt joy of our reunion had subsided a little when my well-tuned female intuition picked up signals that all had not been as it should have been during my six-month absence. With Karen's sisters around it would never be possible for her to keep secrets for too long. We resumed our nights out together, or rather I once more travelled with the family wherever they were playing, whenever I was not working in my new job. I quickly learned that Karen had spent quite a few evenings together with a farmer's son who worked as a labourer in the building trade. What she saw in him I don't know, because he wasn't much to look at. Of course eventually I confronted her. She explained that it was true, but it wasn't serious, she just didn't like to be alone too much and, after all, she was still very young. Now that I was back all would be well, she concluded.

Shortly after my return I had started work in my new hotel. It was not a live-in position as such, though I could stay over when necessary, provided rooms were available, especially when working on late-night functions.

Once more I had to think again about accommodation. As it happened, Karen's granny had a mobile home parked beside the bungalow of one of her daughters, two of whom lived with their families next door to each other. I persuaded her to let me use this, though it was a little dilapidated looking, as it had not been used for quite a while. So I set about sprucing up the old mobile home, which was anything but mobile as it was sitting on concrete blocks. When I was finished cleaning and varnishing, it was a quite homely, though compact, living space.

From here I now commuted the 20-odd miles to my workplace. It would take me 25 or 30 minutes depending on traffic.

In my job as Assistant Manager in the hotel I was really another Jack-of-all-trades. I stood in at the reception when the receptionist was off, I helped set up and prepare for functions such as weddings and dinner dances, I helped out in the bar if the pressure was on there, and at times I was at the ballroom door for the weekly dance, where things could get quite rough at times and brawls could develop very quickly.

When I did stay over occasionally, I would know from the reception which rooms, if any, were available and before long I had figured out a way to make use of rooms which had been booked for the night preceding a wedding-reception the following day. This room would be used for the storage of the going away clothes of bride and groom and bridesmaids and best men. Therefore they were not available to let to other residents, but perfectly okay for me to use the bed after a late night. The room would then be serviced well in time before the wedding party would appear.

They also afforded me an opportunity to once more follow my female instincts and secret desires, and there must be a few brides and bridesmaids who enjoyed their wedding receptions at that hotel, totally oblivious to the fact that I had sampled their fine clothes. I would try them on, and after a few hours of bliss, replace everything as meticulously as ever. Nobody ever had reason for complaint, though I once more had plenty of reasons to doubt who I really was, and what exactly it was that was making me do this. I have to admit that I couldn't help myself.

Given the opportunity of having female clothing around, and the necessary privacy, I couldn't stop myself from succumbing to my inner voice, which was pleading with me to try things on, to bring out what was increasingly heralding itself as the real me. But the pleasure was always fleeting, and tinged with a vague sadness. I knew that standing there as a man, I was in the wrong body for these clothes I still somehow felt most comfortable in.

\*\*\*

My boss decided in spring 1974 that he would no longer require an Assistant Manager and I was due to leave the hotel in mid-March.

At this stage Karen and I had been engaged for well over a year and we decided it was time to get married. We were by no means well off, but determined to make it a special day regardless. The hotel in which I had been working was an excellent wedding venue, with fine mature gardens for the usual wedding photography as well as gracious old world function rooms. I approached my boss and persuaded him to let me have the wedding breakfast at cost price. Maybe he was easily persuaded because of his decision to terminate my employment, but at any rate the wedding meal provided on the day was excellent, and all at just over £1 per head.

In typical Irish fashion, our extended families were invited, and if someone brought their best friend, then another friend of someone else also had to be invited in order not to offend anyone. Second and third cousins, most of them unknown to me, were crawling out of the woodwork and before we knew it there was a guest list of 120. Of those, most were from the bride's side of the family.

Weddings are peculiar; you bring together people from the same families, some of whom can't stand each other and maybe even don't talk to each other. Then you know they will drink plenty of alcohol, and after that you just hope for the best. Even with the small contingent on my side there would be challenges, as both my mother and my father would be there and they were hardly on speaking terms after their divorce two years earlier.

Karen was now busy and excited making plans for the wedding. There was of course that all-important dress to be picked, decisions to be made on who would be bridesmaid and what outfits to get for them, choosing the 'going away' clothes, what kind of flower arrangements and bouquets to have. Karen was in her element. She found the wedding dress she wanted and a lot of the other outfits were hand-made, with patterns and materials of her choice and long hours of hard work and much patience. As for me, I went to

Dublin to find a suit that would be right for my wedding and yet would be cheap at the same time. Looking back at those wedding photos now is a little embarrassing and would be anyway, even if it were not for my completely different life now. But the purple suit with the wide lapels and the pink stitching has to be seen in the context of the age, and at any rate both Karen and I loved all things purple.

For reasons I have never fully understood, there were local people who had taken a real dislike to me and sometimes took it upon themselves to play practical jokes on me. One day, for example, I found the locks of the mobile home, which I had spent much time and effort sprucing up, super-glued.

I was due to finish work in the hotel in mid-March, preceding Easter, and our wedding date had been set for soon after that. In the days leading up to our wedding I stayed in Karen's parents' home and sometime in the night from Holy Thursday to Good Friday my car was doused with battery acid. In the morning, Karen's father came to tell me that the paintwork was lifting off my car. Needless to say we were distraught, because this was now the Easter weekend and we were due to get married in three days and then take off with our car on honeymoon to Germany.

Instead of quietly being able to finish our preparations we were forced to beg the local spray shop to take in our car for another re-spray on Good Friday. That sounds simple, but it required Karen, her brother and me to sand down the car for hours in order for it to be finished in time. Of course there was another fat bill to pay at a time when we already had a lot of expenses due to the wedding. But somehow we made it, no doubt to the chagrin of those responsible for this act of childish, jealous vandalism.

It was Easter Saturday evening before I could drive the car away; there was no hen party for Karen and no stag night for me. The night before the wedding I stayed in a guest house close to the hotel. There I had just a couple of drinks with my brothers, enough to keep myself occupied and not to think too much about the event ahead.

The wedding car was kindly supplied by one of my previous employers, Liam of the Inn, who appeared later at the reception and caused some good-humoured uproar. We had also been able to employ the services of a friend, whose speciality was wedding photography, which would be done at a reasonable cost. Our honeymoon destination would be Germany, where I wanted Karen to get a glance at some of my old haunts.

And so the wedding day came and it was a glorious day, though a cool breeze whistled around the chapel entrance. Later on however, men were in their shirtsleeves as we were blessed with an unusually warm Easter Monday.

The wedding went very well; we had the weather, excellent food, the invited guests, even my estranged parents managed to remain civil. There were no rows, though no doubt plenty of whispered gossip, in other words a pretty typical Irish wedding; except that the groom was dodgy, and German to boot.

We went off that evening with the usual farewells and tears, balloons and other objects tied to our car, as is the custom, and 'Newly Wed' written in pink lipstick all over the bonnet and windows. Instead of heading south straight for Dun Laoghaire, where we were booked into a guest house and from where we were due to catch an early morning car ferry the next day, I found myself heading to Karen's house once more, because I had forgotten the insurance documents for the car. I remember crawling around the attic, where some of my belongings were stored, but I could not find the documents and eventually we just left without them and decided to leave our car marked as it was, as we, rightly as it turned out, assumed that newly weds would not be hassled too much for documents.

By the time we arrived in our guest house lodgings late at night, we were exhausted after a long and memorable day and we fell asleep happily in each other's arms, quite content to postpone the consummation of the marriage until the next day.

*\*\**

Reading a depiction of my happy wedding day might seem odd to some people. Maybe it seems strange even for me to be describing my wedding day, but it was without doubt a significant day in my life, and how can I say I regret it, when after all I married the girl I was in love with and who I hold in high regard? Did we not manage to produce three children we both love dearly from our union? And we managed to get beyond the Silver Wedding milestone.

The very foundation of our union was always flawed, because of my gender identification problems, but then such words were then unknown and meaningless to me.

It would lead to an unusual and at times uneasy alliance as the years progressed. But there was never any intention to deceive. How could I expect anyone to truly know me when I didn't truly know myself?

I made my commitment in best faith and with every intention to love and to cherish till death us do part and I still do love and cherish, even though Karen and I parted some time ago. It was not her fault.

We were a happily married couple; Karen the blushing bride and I the proud groom, and my secrets aside, that is truly how I thought it would stay forever.

# Chapter 12

## The Honeymooners

We caught the ferry the following morning and we drove along roads I had travelled before, but for Karen it was her first big adventure abroad, except for a brief previous visit to Scotland.

We stayed a night in Zandvoort, a Dutch seaside resort I remembered fondly from previous visits, the most memorable of which was just a weekend with friends in 1967, when we had felt so alive and so full of ourselves. Now it seemed so long ago. Some time after that we arrived in my native city and my most vivid memory is of my car finally giving up the ghost with a puff of smoke and a bang right in the middle of the busiest junction in the city centre. The engine had blown a piston; we ended up pushing the car off the junction, parking it and making phone calls to see if anything could be done.

The model was unknown in Germany and all we could do was to sell the remains for 100 Deutschmarks scrap value. We were left stranded and the rest of our honeymoon plans lay in ruins. My mother's cousin offered us the use of her flat for a few days as she was going away on holidays. We gladly accepted the offer and so at least had a base from which to visit some of my old friends and also to plan our return journey.

It was here in Erna's flat that another significant incident took place, which probably gave both of us food for thought.

One evening as we were getting ready for bed, Karen made some remark in jest about the similarity of our clothes. We both had Indian-style embroidered tops which we wore over bell-bottoms, and both had long hair. I can't recall the words, only that I picked up on it, and said I could make myself look very female in no time at all.

It started off light hearted enough as I disappeared into the bathroom for a couple of minutes, while we kept up a teasing conversation from room to room. I stripped out of my own clothes, finding that the top could be worn on its own as a decent but skimpy minidress, and put on some of Karen's tights, before applying some of her make-up. With some foundation, blusher, a little eye shadow and lipstick on, I then combed back my long hair, and with a spray of perfume, the result was quite presentable and certainly gave the desired effect.

When I re-appeared a few minutes later and jumped onto the bed beside Karen, there was a moment's stunned silence, and then Karen slapped me across the face— something she had never done before, and has never done since. It was just an almost involuntary confused reaction to my appearance, which, far from being what began as a silly joke, was far too convincing for Karen's liking.

I guess at that moment she knew that there was more to this than she so far understood or wanted to know, and I knew by her unexpected reaction that I had better change both my clothes, and the subject, quickly. We did our best to laugh it off after that, but I think we also both knew there was more to this than an awkward moment, and neither of us knew how to grasp the opportunity to explore further.

It would be a long time before another similar incident occurred, and I once more learned to bury my confused feelings whenever they arose.

After staying there for a few days and travelling around my native country, we made our way back to England and stopped over for a night with some distant relatives. They sold us an old green Mini at a cheap price, which we then used for the return ferry journey.

Our marriage then had an inauspicious start, with the honeymoon turning out very different from what we had planned, and now we were returning to a new and very uncertain future. My brother and his girlfriend had by then acquired their first house and offered us a room at a fairly low rent, but it did mean sharing bathroom and kitchen facilities. But much worse was having to share a house with thin walls between a newly-wed couple and another couple, whose relationship was at breaking point. No doubt they could hear our subdued couplings through the thin interior stud walls, and we often had to listen to their noisy and passionate arguments.

Karen and I both managed to find employment at a bar and lounge business nearby. Money was very tight and in the end the combination of constant money worries and Karen's frequent homesickness brought this early phase of our marriage to an inevitable end and we returned to the area of her youth one year after our wedding.

***

Having decided to return to Karen's old surroundings we once more had to search for somewhere suitable to live and new jobs to sustain ourselves. We managed to do both relatively quickly and it led to probably one of the best and most peaceful periods of our lives.

Very close to Karen's parents' house, easily overlooked as you drove by, was a small cottage, though even 'cottage' is an exaggeration. A little weekend summer house set back well away from the road, it was accessed through an old iron gate and down a narrow concrete path, with a little strip of lawn either side of the path and a few fruit trees. Adjoining on one side of the property is the old village hall, which was then still used for the occasional dance or the Christmas bazaar and occasional local meetings.

I had made some enquiries and found out that an old lady who then resided in England owned this little property and only visited very rarely. Letters were dispatched and while she was at first not at all keen to let this little house to anyone, the idea of an additional regular little income plus my promise to improve everything at my expense persuaded her in the end.

The little house was in an absolute mess, but we had imagination and the necessary determination and skill to make it into something of a little doll's house. It was our first place to live without the constant presence of others, and it felt like home.

The house had really just two rooms with a tiny scullery and an outside toilet. We didn't mind, because we were always welcome to have a bath in Karen's parents' house and we could also store some belongings there. We resurfaced all the walls with stipple plaster, which hid the cracks and uneven surfaces. Everything was painted bright, a few bits of furniture were brought in, lights and curtains were added, and it quickly became a cosy nest for us.

I approached a number of publicans and was soon offered a managerial job in a town centre pub. I commuted the few miles to work and later Karen came to work there part-time too. The pub was always very busy during the lunch hours and did a very good trade with bar food. Our social life, as with any ordinary couple, consisted of the odd cinema visit or going out to listen to live music sometimes, but often we just stayed in. Karen's sisters would call in passing, but otherwise we did not have a lot of visitors.

*** 

We celebrated our first wedding anniversary, and now lived just around the corner from where we had exchanged our vows. By summer we had settled into somewhat of a routine, but then one day my brother Anthony mentioned that he had an idea to plan for a long and adventurous African trip, organised by one of the specialist overland expedition companies. To prepare for this he would go to London for a year first, both to facilitate all the necessary visas and paperwork, and also to enable him to save the necessary funds.

He had persuaded Harald, my younger brother to join him. I was intrigued; there was an opportunity to fulfil a dream, to see the most fascinating wildlife close up. On the other hand I was married and Karen had been quite homesick during our time in a different part of Ireland, and this time it would not be an option to come home for a weekend.

We must have debated this over a couple of weeks, but Karen could see that being that close to her family meant getting drawn into all the normal family squabbles and disputes. We decided to be adventurous and to go for it. It was a decision that would have many implications for our relationship.

# CHAPTER 13

## AFRICA

A few years after meeting Karen we set off for Africa. There we were 16 people with eight different nationalities, equally divided along the gender lines, or at least we would have been if it hadn't been for me, always capable of upsetting any gender balance.

Africa! When I think of Africa the images just come flooding back; images as fragmented as Africa itself with its colourful multitude of tribal peoples, so poorly led then and now by a long succession of autocrats, tyrants, despots and megalomaniacs like Mobutu, Amin, Bokassa, Banda, Mugabe, building their personal wealth and fiefdoms while robbing their wonderful people of their potential and intensifying their endemic poverty.

When we arrived in Africa, we quickly learned that patience was something we would require plenty of. At the many border crossings we often had to sit patiently for hours before the officials would let us proceed. You might have the vehicle searched by the authorities of the country you were exiting and then again by the border guards of the country you were entering and if you were unlucky you could be stopped again down the road and have the whole procedure repeated by either the army or the police.

Everyone had managed to get all the necessary visas for the entire journey, except for my brother Anthony and myself. We had not succeeded right to the end in London to obtain the required entry visa for Algeria. We had been advised to proceed however, as we would likely be able to obtain a visa from an Algerian embassy or consulate in Morocco. That proved to be bad advice and we did not manage to obtain the necessary visa and thus would not be allowed to proceed into Algeria.

We now had a major problem. If you look at the map of Africa, you see that Algeria is a huge country, large parts of course straddling the Sahara with its most inhospitable terrain. After much discussion with the rest of the group Anthony and I reluctantly decided to meet up again two weeks later at the main post office in Agadez, a town in the north of the Republic of Niger, when the truck would be due to arrive. We also arranged that if we were there first we would wait and if possible send signals with other Over Landers travelling in the opposite direction.

At the same time Mark, the official tour guide, promised to send messages to the post office in Agadez with faster moving vehicles going south to keep us informed of their progress. It was particularly difficult for me, because I had to leave Karen in very uncertain circumstances, though I knew she would be safe with the group. We had not been apart since getting married and this was not a part of the adventure we had envisaged.

\*\*\*

Anthony and I had a long and arduous two weeks, full of scares and surprises, but eventually we managed to reunite with the others. It was time for an emotional reunion, but though I was of course immensely relieved to be together once more with Karen, I sensed soon enough that something was amiss. We were glad to be part of the camp set-up again, sleeping once more with a roof over our heads, even if it was only a tent and getting our share of the communal meal.

Over that evening's fire there was much exchange of our adventures and theirs during our two-week separation, but still I felt a certain reticence among the group—something was being held back.

Later, as most were heading for their tents, I finally got some time alone with Karen and I found out what had happened. Various people had paired off in our absence; one couple had fallen in love, a relationship which developed into marriage, and they still live happily married in Australia today.

Mark had struck up a more casual relationship with a Danish girl, but what really devastated me was that Karen, my wife for just two and a half years, had betrayed me with Karl, the mechanic and driver.

It was a real blow for me. Here I had been separated from the girl I loved so much and instead of the pure joy of being reunited I now had to face this betrayal and the knowledge that the whole group was aware of this tryst. No wonder I had immediately sensed tension.

Karen was very sorry and tried to explain how difficult it was to be alone on such a trip, and how she couldn't cope with it, but for me it was an inexcusable breach of loyalty and trust. I had only been gone for two weeks, and she knew

I would be coming back to the group. There was such a confusion of feelings for me; anger, frustration, jealousy, a sense of betrayal and worthlessness. It was a very severe emotional crisis during a very trying if adventurous period alone.

What stands out once more for me is my reaction to this seemingly unbearable news. As so often at times of real crisis in my life, I withdrew into the safety of my inner female self. I crawled into the tent and got dressed in a wonderful long, hooded white caftan with purple stitching around the top, which Karen had bought for herself in Morocco. I curled up in the foetal position and I cried into my pillow, to muffle the sound and to hide my pain from those in the other tents nearby.

Protected from the outer world, and safely ensconced within my inner sanctum, I could at last come to terms with what had happened, and grieve. Karen eventually came and comforted me, and as we lay together in the tent she saw my inner self emerge, and I feel that a deeper understanding developed between us as a result.

Not for the first time, and certainly not for the last, I had to seriously doubt Karen's sense of commitment and loyalty in our relationship, but also once more I had reason to ask myself who I really was. Was I, as her husband, not the man she wanted? Was it because of my other side that she sought out the company of other men? It was a long and sad night, though Karen assured me this affair was over and she managed to comfort me to sleep eventually. I did confront Karl, with Karen also present, as soon as I got an opportunity to get him alone, without others around. He too was apologetic and a bit sheepish about the whole affair, and promised it would not happen again. On one occasion a few days later I did find the two of them talking alone together and it was like an arrow of jealousy going through my heart.

They assured me nothing more was going on. I guess I could have ended our marriage in those days, but effectively I could not have left—we both needed to stay with the group to complete the journey. There was no escape in a way, but in reality, whatever about my most inner feelings, I also loved Karen and was not willing to give up on us so easily.

***

Africa was the most amazing trip of my life, but the wonderful memories of that year will always be tinged with sadness because of this betrayal.

It wasn't easy, but soon we had to get up and get on with things, and I knew that I had no choice but to carry on, and after a while Karen and I grew closer again.

Our adventures included an amazing encounter with a pygmy hunting party, deep in the rainforests of Cameroon. In the very heart of Africa we slept beneath the walls of the palace built by one of the African megalomaniacs of the day, the self-appointed Emperor Bokassa.

There were more incidents to be had involving wildlife, such as when I decapitated a snake which had managed to get into one of our tents, and the time I was charged by an elephant when I had tried to get a photo at close range, and on foot. Thankfully the elephant didn't think I was worth the pursuit.

We covered about 10,000 miles through 15 African countries, of which about two thirds had been on dirt roads. Instead of the planned 18 weeks our journey had taken almost five months of adventurous and often arduous travelling. We had learned a lot about what had been an unknown world to us and, more importantly, we had learned a lot about ourselves.

We ended up in South Africa where we needed to find work to afford our journey home, and stayed for three months earning our plane tickets back.

But even the best adventures must come to a close and after months of travelling, came the shock announcement, which I could not immediately digest and comprehend.

One day, while I was busy playing an intense game of table tennis, Karen came into the room and dropped the bombshell that she thought she was pregnant. I think she has never quite forgiven me for just continuing to play the game to the end, but I guess I just couldn't take it in.

We were to have a child and that would change our lives without doubt. We would have to settle down for sure now; our gypsy days had to come to an end.

We made plans to go home and finally, a few weeks later, we boarded the plane for the long flight northwards, even more like a family than when we had left. I was still going through the same confusing feelings within me, and had even displayed my feminine side when I had felt hurt, but now, once more, my masculine side was taking over. I had my wife back, and now, I was about to become a father.

In the end it wasn't the thousands of miles travelled on dirt roads, it was the parallel inner journey, which left its indelible mark on all of us.

# CHAPTER 14

## STEPHEN

Once we returned and got over the changes that had occurred in our absence we had to find accommodation and suitable employment as soon as possible.

We looked around for a flat or house to rent and eventually found a largely unoccupied mansion, which had been sub-divided into a number of flats. The large brick building sits well back from the street in a demesne of tall trees and bushes. We found the owner, a lady who owned a pub in a nearby village, and persuaded her to let us have one of the unoccupied flats. Some time later Karen's sister and her husband followed us there and took another flat on the other side of the house.

There were only two other flats occupied at the time we moved there, one by a charming old lady, quite deaf and rarely seen, and the other by Frank and his wife, an elderly couple living in the ground floor flat. We would be moving into the one above them. They were lovely neighbours and we never had any cross words with them.

The flat and the whole building were in a poor state of repair and we tried to get the landlady to undertake some repairs, particularly various small leaks, but the promises were never fulfilled and we simply stopped paying rent in the end, which did not seem to perturb her either. We did the best to make the flat as comfortable as possible with some assistance from Karen's parents, who gave us bits of furniture. Entry to the flat was by means of a steep set of outside stairs and the flat consisted of no less than five rooms, two of which we never used as they were in need of major work. The whole flooring was suffering from dry rot and needed replacing. We ended up with a living room with a small kitchen corner, a small sitting room and our bedroom.

As always our combined DIY skills converted what had been an almost completely uninhabitable mess into a reasonable living space. There was one additional problem though; even though there were only five human inhabitants, there were plenty of uninvited guests of the four-legged variety.

With a nearby grain store and spillages of grain along the road throughout the harvest season, rats had a great food supply and the partially empty building offered a great sanctuary for them. We kept the doors to the two rooms we were not using firmly shut most of the time, because there were obvious rat holes in the timber floor and you could hear the patter of tiny feet often enough. My brother and I set up a fishing line under the closed door with a bit of bacon on a hook and we didn't have to wait too long before we could feel a good tug on the line. We didn't manage to hook that specimen but on another day Karen opened the door to empty a bin and was confronted by a large rat, obviously full of poison, that keeled over at her feet. So you could say our circumstances were far from ideal, but we had little money and could only move to better quarters as our circumstances allowed.

To pay even the very modest rent required here we needed work to avoid frittering away the £1,000 we had managed to save in South Africa. We looked around but there was little on offer and so we came up with the idea of buying a chip van and making our living by going to dancehalls and other outdoor events, selling fast food for a living.

We did find a fairly rickety Ford Transit, which had been converted into a chip van, and bought it for £800. We had the van re-sprayed, some repairs carried out, and displayed in bold proud letters on the front and above the hatch the name of our first business. We learned as we went along, making plenty of mistakes at the beginning, but knowing soon what sold and where to go and where not to go. It was a hard life and after each night out you smelled like a soggy fried chip, but there were weeks when we made a good living. Our best night was usually Sunday night at the ballroom where I had first gone dancing.

We would arrive early to set up, get the gas-fired chip pans going, pre-fry chips and fish, and organise as best we could for the rush ahead. While the dance was on there would just be a steady trickle of customers, but once we heard the National Anthem being played we had to be prepared for all hell to break loose. An avalanche of people would surround the van. It was a challenge to keep up with the orders.

We had to do so many chips that it would be hard to keep the pans hot and I shudder at the thought of what went out for food at times, probably much of it spewed up later along with the excess alcohol consumed. Still, this was our main money earner and we could clear £100 in a night; a lot in those days. On some Saturday nights we would sit in the main street though here we faced more competition and takings were usually modest. We would look at the local papers and see what was on and then prepare and hope for the best.

There were nights when we had stones thrown at us in a village. Violence was always a risk when serving a multitude of impatient and often drunken customers. We carried a couple of large spanners used mainly for changing the large gas-tanks, but also if necessary for protection. There was also the night when totally exhausted, I nodded off on the icy steep hill and we slid sideways down the road, lucky not to overturn the vehicle. We would arrive home very late in the morning and fall into our beds exhausted, and then face cleaning up the stinking van the next day.

Sometimes it was just Karen and I, but on the big nights my brother Harald and Michelle, then Karen's brother's girlfriend worked with us. It was never easy, but we made a living and we were independent. Karen worked right up to the time when she barely fitted in the chip van with our son's imminent arrival.

*** 

It was indeed with the chip van that I finally brought Karen to the hospital. It must have been a sight for all to see. Karen gave birth to our only son, Stephen. It was a difficult birth. Not being well off, we had not booked a doctor, knowing that if there should be any emergency a doctor would be called anyway. Stephen didn't seem too willing to leave the comfort of the womb and it took forceps to persuade him in the end, which left his head a little misshapen for a couple of days.

No wonder it had been a difficult birth, with the baby weighing in at over nine pounds. We were both proud of our first child and we were soon able to take him home in his wicker basket, which would be his bed for the next weeks and months. Throughout the first winter months we had many sleepless nights with Stephen as he suffered badly with croup, possibly caused by the damp condition of the flat. We would get up in turns, boil the kettle and have the room filled with steam until Stephen would settle down once more and his asthmatic wheezing would stop.

In spite of his little health problems Stephen developed into a feisty little character, quite capable of throwing noisy tantrums when things did not go his way. When I look at pictures of him now at about a year old, he looks like a cheeky Dennis the Menace character; lots of freckles, a little cap and a cheeky grin. He still has those qualities today and I love him for it.

It was becoming more and more apparent though, that the means of our livelihood, our chip van, was becoming more and more unreliable, with frequent breakdowns leading to loss of earnings at the very time when our requirements were growing with our new family member. It was high time to look for new means of income. By now I liked the idea of independence and working for myself and also wanted to do something together with Harald, my younger brother, because he had gotten used to earning some money from the chip van too.

My mother had always dabbled a little bit in antiques, buying and selling the likes of brassware and pewter, porcelain and some silver. She would sell at reasonable profits to her German guests, who always seemed interested in old Irish bric-a-brac. We decided to invest whatever we could spare into buying such items and then taking them by car to Germany, where we would sell them profitably to small antiques dealers. First refusal we would give to my uncle who operated a small antiques shop in a tourist and spa town on the Rhine.

By then I had bought an old Escort Estate car, which we used to go around antique shops in the surrounding counties to find suitable items, mostly quite small, such as candle sticks, clocks, oil lamps and silver or pewter tea sets. We made a couple of trips and managed to sell enough to make a small profit, but already it was evident that it would be difficult to make this business work on such a small scale with the relatively high costs of ferry tickets and fuel, food and accommodation while travelling. On one trip the axle on our car shifted due to the excess weight of our goods, and this in turn led to break failure. I ran into the rear of another vehicle, fortunately at crawling pace, on a jammed motorway. The ensuing repair was another major setback, and then during our last trip we were asked by German customs to pull over and they interrogated us for hours and demanded payment of 1,500 Deutschmarks for outstanding duties on our cargo. We were shocked, as we had understood that antiques were duty-free. It turned out to be true, but only if we could prove everything to be over 100 years old.

We couldn't, and quite obviously some of our stuff was later than the Victorian period. We had carried everything quite openly and had no intention of defrauding customs. Each article was coded with a label, which would help us later in determining the correct selling price in the shops. Now the customs officers wanted to see our books to explain the coding and that is how they calculated the duty we had to pay.

We didn't have the money to pay and we faced seizure of everything. We had no choice in the end but to ring my uncle, who agreed to travel to the border with the necessary funds to get us as well as our goods released. Of course he would expect repayment in kind as he was above all a shrewd businessman. We went to his shop eventually and knowing our situation, he pressed us to sell many of the items to him at almost no profit to us.

We came back from this trip dispirited. My brother would have to find his own way and my dream of independence seemed over for now. Importantly, I needed to find work as soon as possible to look after my family. After all, I was the man of the house; the breadwinner.

Throughout this period my internal dilemmas remained mostly just that—internal. I tried my best to suppress my inner desires and feelings, and the female voice that seemed to be screaming out from within. I had to focus on being the man I outwardly was; the husband and father the world saw me for.

There were some occasions when I would secretly experiment with Karen's things, though that was not easy because our sizes did not match too well. Also, we were now a little family and I tried hard to suppress any wayward thoughts, and tried to convince myself that all would be well if only I tried harder. I mean, for God's sake, had I not fallen in love with a girl, married the girl and now had fathered a child? How could I still dream of being a woman?

# Chapter 15

## High Flying Act

Christmas 1978 was not a happy time for us. It was obvious that we could not continue with the antiques trading, as our resources were totally insufficient to buy in big enough volumes to make individual trips worthwhile, especially now that we had to allow for the considerable slice customs would take from us on anything not proven to be over 100 years old. Also the old Escort Estate was in no fit state to survive more trips heavily laden with goods, and I didn't have the money to replace it with a more reliable means of transport.

No matter how we looked at it, there were no longer ways and means to stay independent, as we just did not have any capital or the credit to start a new venture. So, very reluctantly, I had to start looking for a job once more. January 1979 was a bad time to be looking for work in Ireland. The economy had stagnated and there was a lot of unemployment. The service industry in which I had some considerable experience by now was in its traditionally lowest ebb between Christmas and Easter, but I was not very keen to go back there anyway.

Scrutinising the papers, I saw an ad promising an opportunity with rather opaque language, not really telling you what it was about. Truth be told, had it said clearly that they were looking for sales people working on a self-employed basis on commission only, I would never have applied.

The first interview would lead me into a career that saw me progressing rapidly upwards, leading to my most successful decade, at least in monetary terms. I was offered a two-week residential training course in Dublin, to commence in early February 1979.

There is no doubt in my mind that it was the very fact that I had nothing to lose and everything to gain if I were to succeed that made me do it. I got through the sales course with flying colours, graduated along with 14 others from the sales class, and was ready to be field trained by my area manager by the end of the course.

The company I had joined was the Irish subsidiary of a huge multinational company, now expanding sales of their low-cost healthcare products into Europe. Essentially the company had little to lose, other than investing the costs of training and some sales material for each new representative. The onus for success was very much on the individual and that is why the rate of attrition for new recruits was always high. Within just a few weeks I was the only one still in the field of the group of 14 who had trained with me, but I would stay with the company and rise through the ranks for the next eight and a half years, winning many awards along the way.

\*\*\*

When I look back, especially at these early days, I am amazed at myself and at the success I achieved, but in the end selling is largely acting—the better an actor you are, the more convincingly you sell your product—and I had been a successful actor all my life. I had always lived as someone I projected myself to be; a man from Germany who had come to Ireland, married, and started a family—a normal, family man. Only I knew the truth at the core of myself. Now as my career in a very male-dominated business took off rapidly, my act became ever more convincing and it is little wonder that those who learned the truth about me so many years later, when I was finally forced to let my mask slip, were so shocked and couldn't really comprehend what I was telling them.

This company was the right vehicle for me at this time, because I was hungry for success after my earlier failures, and I really wanted to improve things for our family. With the clever system of awards and incentives the company operated in typical multi-national fashion. I had lots of little stepping-stones to success. Sales success largely depended on achieving 100 new sales units each week, and I managed to do this for 29 consecutive weeks, by which time I had already been promoted into the first junior sales management role. I learned how important your own attitude is in determining success.

The rewards for this success was an immediate high income I achieved on a week-to-week basis, along with many prizes and sales awards, usually presented at large regional sales meetings where you could share your success stories with others to help motivate them and yourself to aim even higher.

The price you paid for this success was a loss of family life, as you spent long hours knocking on doors to people who very often were anything but pleased to see a cold-calling sales person. In my time I was threatened with a pitchfork, a shotgun and many dogs. However, I did manage to go through my whole sales career without ever being bitten. Or shot.

For the first time we were saving in a serious way in a building society. Soon I bought our first new car, a black Mazda 323, albeit with the help of hire purchase. Then we could afford a second used car for Karen to give her more independence during my long days out selling. I would later lose this car in a hijacking by the IRA, when I was pulled over at a fake border check and watched with some alarm as a masked man who was far more nervous than I was held me at gunpoint until he and his associates drove off.

After a few months I was promoted to senior area manager with an enlarged territory. It now meant driving a little further from home, spending even more time away. The income grew with additional override commissions on the sales of my team, but the personal price I paid also grew. On the one hand our personal living standard improved rapidly, but on the other hand Karen and I had little enough time to enjoy our newfound wealth.

It was around this time that we first met Philip and Stephanie, who would become our long-term friends. There was an immediate bond, particularly with Philip and Karen's shared interest in music, as both played in bands. We started going to gigs where Philip was playing, whenever we had the time, and we were soon spending many weekends together.

Philip, without doubt, was very easy to get on with and he could keep us going with jokes all night long. Karen and Stephanie soon developed a close friendship.

We spent a lot of time together and shared a number of foreign holidays. Philip and I shared interests in sport, though in other ways we were very different.

\*\*\*

We had now bought our very first home; a three-bedroom bungalow with a small front garden area with our own double-gated drive-through and a sizeable lawn area at the rear. It was just a few miles from the village where Karen had spent all her youth and within a short distance of all her family, with whom she could spend time during my long hours of absence in my demanding job.

Now I was even busier, working all the hours I could, and then in my time at home there was a house to be re-decorated and a garden to be looked after. We had come a long way in just about three years, starting out with a damp flat in a rat-infested building with no savings and a battered old car to a two-car family with a bungalow in the country.

It was all built on an opportunity offered and grabbed by me with both hands. We now changed our cars annually, not totally surprising since I was doing enormous mileage every year. Our house was nicely decorated, we managed to get out usually on Saturdays for a meal or to listen to a band somewhere, and we started having annual holidays in places like Spain, the Canary Islands and Tunisia.

I had truly joined the rat race with an ever-increasing living standard, though not necessarily an enriched living experience. By now I was so good at convincing everyone of Paul Grieg, the successful businessman, that I even convinced myself. When my inner doubts about my identity inevitably surfaced from time to time, I managed to suppress them. There was too much at stake for me to start getting distracted by confusing thoughts of who I really was and what I wanted to be.

So much of my life centred around work, with all its stress, that come the weekend, it was difficult for me to get up the enthusiasm for going out. But I usually did, aware that Karen was always keen to go out as she spent too much time in the house while I worked.

Materialistically speaking this episode in my life was no doubt the most successful, but spiritually probably the most impoverished.

By 1983 I was promoted once more; now I was a district manager with a team of area managers under me, teaching them how to become successful in their jobs.

\*\*\*

One particular sales meeting once more highlighted my underlying insecurity, which by and large I covered so well. We used to have major sales meetings about four times a year, which would invariably be followed by major sales weeks with all manner of attempts at record-breaking. Every region, district and area, and the individuals who worked them, would strive to break their records, always stretching themselves to greater achievement.

The concept of Valentine's Day was to be used as a tool to motivate the sales people to make even greater efforts for their 'sweethearts'. This year, it was decided that, to add an element of fun, all the male district managers should dress up as women. I tried as casually as I could to persuade the group to come up with another idea, but they thought it would be a great laugh, and I didn't want to be seen to protest too much, because that would only lead to further scrutiny and the predictable, 'What are you afraid of?' jibes.

Personally, I was terrified of somehow showing too much of my true nature, and perhaps appearing too convincing, too close for comfort. When the day came, there must have been some 600 people assembled in the hotel ballroom where the meeting was being held. In due course the district managers, who had been busy preparing for their grand entrance, were called onto the stage and invited to go through the aisles to show the available incentive merchandise for the week ahead. All the other district managers had dressed in the caricature mode probably expected by both management and the crowd. I, on the other hand, strangely with Karen's help, had gone for a pretty convincing, if slightly raunchy, female look, with a wig, a black dress to just below the knee, high heels and black stockings with suitable make-up and jewellery.

There were plenty of wolf whistles, but inside I was mortified at showing somehow how I truly felt. Here they were congratulating me on my successful take-off of a slightly saucy female, while in reality I wanted to scream, 'That's who I really am.' Or at least, who I wanted to be.

I was glad when it was all over and I could hide once more in my business suit and my really convincing take-off of the successful businessman. It was ironic that I was far more comfortable changing back into what I considered a costume than I was wearing what I thought were the right clothes for me.

There were other occasions, when we went to fancy dress balls, where the chance to dress up was presented to me. I wonder if people ever noticed that my costume always seemed to have a female theme. On one particular occasion, where everyone in our party had made a really good effort, I appeared as half male, half female, with a cunning outfit made with the help of Karen, who also made up the right side of my face. Everything was split right down the middle.

People congratulated me on the original idea, but they couldn't see what I was silently screaming at them. I was a tortured contradiction on legs; one leg slightly longer than the other due to the difference in heel size. I had chosen my right side as the female side and I was sub-consciously saying, 'This is my right side.'

I wanted to be found out and yet was terrified in case I was. No doubt Karen could at times guess at my inner turmoil and anguish—after all, she was always willing to help with the dress-up, which was perhaps her way of showing support—but avoided talking about it. It was just a situation that we felt we had to avoid talking about; instead pretending that it was all in the name of fun—just dressing up and putting on a show.

Every now and then situations like these would arise, but by and large I succeeded in suppressing my inner self, and the woman within was almost strangled by neglect and by my own fears.

Karen always liked those big sales meetings as it gave her the best chance to show off her wardrobe while mixing with the other sales manager's wives, having a good time in good hotels with fine food and plenty to drink. It was a chance for her to enjoy the success.

\*\*\*

Stephen was by now going to the primary school and we felt that it was time for him to have a brother or sister. By that autumn Karen was pregnant once more and all seemed to be going well. One day while I was attending a senior management meeting in our Dublin head office, I was called to the phone. On the other end was a very excited Karen; she had just found out during a hospital check-up that she was expecting twins.

I too was now infected with her excitement and joy and had to tell everyone in the room why I had been called to the phone. It was a most exciting time. We were endlessly planning and at the same time wondering how we would cope with two new babies in the house.

That year seemed like the very pinnacle of success; first there was the marvellous news about the twins due to arrive sometime in the summer and then the company, having decided to re-arrange the division of the company from two regions into three, decided that I was the best choice for the position of third regional sales manager based on the excellent sales results achieved within my district. To top it off, I was nominated for an international sales award which was presented to me in Europe.

Looking back, I realise that I reached these levels of success under false pretences. I was being feted as Paul Grieg and yet I frequently felt like a fraud, because that was not who I felt I was. But sadly I could not have reached the same level of success as the person I really am, Paula Grieg.

The other obvious thing is that while my inner, female side was screaming out, I was set to become a father again, this time to twins, and I couldn't have been a prouder man.

During the summer I brought Karen to the hospital for what was meant to be another check-up. But that morning she was kept in and at 3pm my first daughter Sally appeared. Just 15 minutes later her twin sister Clare also made an appearance.

I stayed throughout the birth and it will always be one of the most treasured experiences of my life. Karen of course had to bear the brunt, but she bore up bravely. Though I witnessed the event I am sad sometimes that I will never know that painful joy of giving birth.

Both children were healthy, with a combined weight of more than 12lbs, and Stephen was also proud of his twin sisters, though he must at times have felt suddenly demoted with everyone fussing over them.

There is no doubt that our lives changed drastically, as Karen took on most of the work of looking after two demanding babies. When two babies cry at once, want feeding, want changing, want attention, it can be exhausting. I did what I could when I was there, but the demands of my job meant that more often than not I was not.

When I was at home I tried to help with the feeding at night, which especially for Sally was always a prolonged effort. She ate little and often and I can remember vividly sitting slumped into the pillow in my bed, nodding off with exhaustion while rubbing her back to get her wind up. I can't say if my urges towards my children were more maternal or paternal, but I knew that I loved them with every heartbeat and I wanted to protect them and provide for them.

Watching the two of them play and interact, it was possible from quite early on to see that they had both very individual personalities, and they still have today. They look like sisters, but anyone who doesn't know will not take them for twins, not just because of their difference in height, but because they have such different interests as well. To everyone at that time, we must have seemed the perfect couple, blessed with lovely children, living in a nice house, driving two cars, and all built on my good executive position. Yet my 'perfection' wasn't even skin deep.

It was around this time our marital relationship became even more complicated. We used to regularly visit my younger brother. My brother, his wife, Karen and I would go out on a Saturday night together. First we would go for a couple of drinks and then we would split up. My brother and I would go to play snooker in a pub and the girls would head off to have a few drinks elsewhere.

When pub closing came, my brother and I would return home but the girls would stay in town and return later, often much later, by taxi. They would have gone on to a disco or club. I never asked too many questions, even when Karen would come home many hours after the nightclub would have closed.

So it was then, in the early 1980s, that an unspoken agreement somehow took shape. I left Karen with a lot of leeway, and in return she allowed my suffocating other half a little air, which meant she could come home and at times find a woman in her bed, in as much as I could be that woman at that time.

It might sound strange when I say that I can't remember the first time that I dressed up and waited for Karen to come home. It seemed to happen quite seemlessly. I started wearing some silky underwear more often, and then I started experimenting with shaving off the body hair I detested. This would initially lead to many a frightful shaving rash, but I got more adept at it and my skin became more tolerant.

Karen wouldn't necessarily be surprised at my appearance when she returned because sometimes she would leave out a specific complete outfit for me to wear, which gave me at least some feeling of acceptance.

It's strange, but again we didn't talk it out and it wasn't planned; it just happened, and evolved from there. This is what I mean by unspoken agreement; I would not ask too many probing questions of how or where she might have spent the last few hours, and in return she did not ask why exactly I was presenting myself in a progressively more female manner.

I would lie in bed waiting, often for hours, with a terrifying mix of emotions—fear, sadness, and yet excitement, and also love. That was the important thing; I did still love Karen as any husband loves his wife. For me, nothing had changed. What emotions went through Karen's mind when she returned to find me waiting, I don't know, but if it bothered her, she had the good grace not to show it.

Next day I usually went back to pretending all was 'normal' and got on with my daily life and chores. There would be no mention of my dressing as a woman.

No doubt it was then that I should have talked about where this was leading and what was happening to me, but I didn't.

Maybe we were both afraid of facing up to our situation. We were still a loving couple, and we had three beautiful children, so our marriage was still very much real, and neither of us saw our developing relationship as being a threat to our marriage.

Every relationship demands compromise, doesn't it? But if you compromise too much you end up, well, just compromised. For me I was torn between the woman I loved and the woman I increasingly felt I needed to be, and I wrestled with all of my mixed emotions. Having started to let my inner self out, I knew it wasn't enough. I had given my inner self a taste of freedom and now I wanted more, though I made sure that Karen knew nothing.

The feelings inside me were too strong to be satisfied by these occasional experiments with my femininity, but these same feelings were causing me untold confusion. I was a happily married man with a family, so why was I feeling like this? What exactly was it that I was feeling?

Today, if you're not sure about something you Google it. But back then it was only in the mid-80s that I first came across an advertisement in a UK newspaper for special services for transgendered people, which then started me off looking out for newspaper articles about these issues. The article provided dressing services for transvestites and transsexuals. I started to learn more about my situation and found that it had a name, which led me to further investigate everything about it and come to some realisations. I had never heard this terminology before but I knew instantly that I belonged to this group of people.

At first, I didn't know whether I was a transvestite or a transsexual. I enjoyed dressing as a woman, I enjoyed having sex as a woman, which fits into the transvestite category. For transvestites, dressing as a woman is a sexual fetish. After they orgasm, they are happy to go back to living as a man. For me it was more than that. When I changed back into men's clothes, I felt as if I was hiding my true self. The fact that I hated my male genitalia was a key factor in identifying my condition. Finally, I came to realise the truth about myself: I was transsexual.

Probably around then I should maybe have considered counselling. But while things were improving somewhat in the UK for transsexuals—after the disastrous electro-shock therapies of the 70s—in Ireland, as far as I was aware then, those kinds of services did not exist. I think that there is still little of this 'expertise' today in Ireland.

One other strange and maybe slightly bizarre footnote is that not long after the birth of the twins we decided that three should be enough; probably a wise decision, and so I had the necessary operation to make sure Karen did not fall pregnant again. Now, as the woman I am today, I wonder how many women can say that they have had a vasectomy!

\*\*\*

From a business point of view the reorganisation in the company had not worked well. Three regions had not brought the desired growth in 1984 and it was decided to revert back to the old division with two regions. As my region had only achieved minimal growth and I had also been the most recently appointed regional manager, I would be left in limbo. My options would have been to once more take up a district manager's position, but the only one on offer would be miles from all our connections, especially Karen's family, and she needed that support network with the three young children and my long absences.

There was one other offer—to move to another area and report to the regional manager who worked as part of the UK company.

Soon I realised that it made more sense to move the family, as it would reduce my endless travelling somewhat and we would live very close to our constant friends, Philip and Stephanie, with whom we still shared most of our social lives.

At the same time Karen had a car, so it was still easy for her to visit friends and family. And so we sold our first house and a new chapter started in Northern Ireland, just as a new chapter had started in my own private life.

# CHAPTER 16

## NORTHERN IRELAND

We decided not to buy a house at once, but rather to rent our accommodation. We found a three-bedroom bungalow in good repair with a very plain garden area.

Throughout our 18-month period in this new area I spent some time in Northern Ireland, where the 'Troubles' were an unwelcome backdrop to our lives. There was constant activity by helicopters, necessary though annoying checkpoints by military patrols, and a few incidents too close for comfort. One day Stephen had just left to go to a friend's house around the corner and we heard a bomb going off nearby. Luckily Stephen had already reached his friend's house, but was still frightened by the vibrations from the device. A few sheep were the only victims this time. On another day on the nearby main Dublin to Belfast road, a judge and his wife were blown up on their return from a foreign holiday.

Once returning from a nearby village soldiers warned me not to proceed, as there was a suspected bomb beneath the railway viaduct. I talked my way through them and had just enough space to drive between the viaduct wall and the abandoned tanker standing there. Later on the evening news they showed the same vehicle and said a large bomb had been defused.

Another morning while staying there we were not allowed to leave our house and soldiers lay behind our garden walls with guns at the ready. More than any of these specific incidents it was the air of suspicion that pervaded the area that really got to us. Strangers in particular were treated with caution, but even among locals you always felt that people knew more than they let on about what was happening, but knew better than to talk about it. There would just be whispers and insinuations. It was not an atmosphere I wanted my children to grow up in. A relatively small number of activists supported by sympathisers—and you could never be sure who they were—managed to control the whole community through fear. I felt I understood what it must have been like for my parent's generation, fearful of the Gestapo and their unknown eyes and ears.

Work-wise my move north proved to be a mistake. Where I had expected a well organised company set-up, I only found a badly led shambles and I soon became disillusioned with it, doing the bare minimum needed.

\*\*\*

Consequent events showed that idle hands and idle minds are not necessarily a good thing, because it was around this time that I had an affair.

Writing about it does not fill me with pride, and invariably these affairs are usually destructive in the end.

Born out of a hotchpotch of frustrated desire, it laid the foundations of tempestuous sexual relationships, which overwhelmed me for a while.

Karen and I found ourselves, on one occasion, out with an acquaintance of mine and a group of his friends. This was August, the height of summer, and there was an air of joviality about the night in question.

We visited some of the bars in a small town, which were all packed, and as a crowd, wandered along the streets between them. Karen and a few other women who had come along were getting merry and were engrossed in an animated conversation with one of the men. Karen started to blatantly flirt with one of the men in the company, making it perfectly obvious to everyone in the group what she was doing. The man in question even looked at me in confusion, with a perplexed look. I could feel a quiet rage starting to build inside me. While I tolerated and even understood her need for other men's company, given that I was dressing as a woman more frequently, I was infuriated that she would rub my nose in it so to speak.

While she was busy, I ended up talking to another woman who felt a little left out of the conversations amongst the main crowd. We were on the way back to our car and Karen was still preoccupied with her conversation that she fell way behind this woman and I, who were walking ahead. There were crowds milling around and suddenly, on impulse, I pulled her into a gap in a wall and kissed her. She did not resist and returned my kiss, and from that beginning an affair was launched which was to last for many months and threaten both of our marriages.

We had all had a few drinks, though I cannot and will not claim that as an excuse for myself. It was an act of momentary self-indulgence, followed by the realisation that this woman was keen to explore further.

After our initial kiss it was obvious that neither of us wanted to leave it at that and before the others had caught up with us, still oblivious and preoccupied with each other, we had arranged to meet the following day. It became quite awkward there and then because we actually knew each other already and had to maintain our appearance of being ordinary friends.

It is astonishing that Karen did not find out on that very night what was happening. Perhaps her trust in me was so complete that she did not contemplate the possibility.

If I do feel bad about these events, it is particularly for Karen, whom I betrayed. Of course I also regret how all of this affected my marriage and the trust essential for any relationship, which, once damaged, is so hard to rebuild. But it is also true that all of this may never have happened, but for my feeling so obviously left out of the day's fun.

There is another aspect which has often exercised my mind about these events. What did it mean to me with regard to my very secret personal female desires? How was this behaviour compatible with these inner emotions? But whatever about my well-hidden doubts about who I was, the fact is that I was then also under the powerful influence of testosterone, providing me with a strong sex drive. But that which was provided by the powerful male sex hormone was then being emasculated by other powerful contradictory signals in my mind. Though I was, physically, perfectly able to function sexually as a man, the processes going on in my mind while doing so were usually anything but male.

From that very first feverish encounter with this other woman, it was clear to me that this was the kind of woman

I had sexually dreamed about and desired; a woman not in any way inhibited and quite happy to usurp the leading role, a strong dominant female, very attractive to me sexually, though often most aggravating in everyday situations. I never fell in love with her, but I certainly fell in lust with her.

Looking back with the distance of many years, it is obvious that we were all betrayed by this affair. There was obviously the woman's husband. There was Karen, who probably had thought me incapable of such events. And then there were my children, who must have felt betrayed when they learned of the affair years later and who now had to look at me in a different light. Maybe even the woman herself was also betrayed, because she did not have the affair with the person who she thought she was having the affair with. Though I had hinted at some of my desires, she did not react in any specific way, nor do I think she ever comprehended to what extent I was using our lovemaking to give vent to my inner frustrations and desires.

And so finally, I betrayed myself. Where once I had married with dignity and honour, saved by ignorance of my condition, I had now engaged in another relationship based on a lie about myself, rather than facing up to the true me. I knew well why I was getting into this affair, but this woman did not. I deceived her in a selfish attempt to feel more feminine, because it was easier to do that than confront my confusion.

With hindsight it is also quite astonishing how we got away for so long with our secret trysts. As stated earlier, by then I had become quite disillusioned with my work; I would go off in the mornings, meet a sales team and its manager, going through the motions, but quite often I had free afternoons to arrange meetings. Arriving too often at her house was another matter entirely. The neighbours would no doubt note my arrivals, and would presumably take note of the fact that I was a man, not the woman's husband, calling on a regular basis.

I guess, as with most of these illicit relationships, it is the fear factor of discovery that makes it all the more exciting at the time. We did also arrange meetings elsewhere and that too led to at least one embarrassing situation. We had arranged to meet at a local beauty spot, usually deserted during the week, up a mountain very close to the border at the edge of the forest. We were heavily engaged and oblivious to our surroundings, when we got a knock on the car door. We hastily grabbed whatever we could to cover ourselves and opened the window. We were surrounded by a British Army patrol, which no doubt had by now checked out the car registrations and had a good idea who we were and what we were doing. They were on anti-terrorist patrol with their camouflage uniforms and painted faces, and no doubt going by the smirks on some of their faces we had provided them with some enjoyable diversion. Thanks to steamy windows they probably did not see that much.

\*\*\*

During that eventful year, other events were beginning to influence me. A couple of visits during the year to my mother at Beech Mount made me aware that she was really struggling on two fronts; firstly with her own health, never good at the best of times, and secondly, she was struggling with my sister.

We didn't visit often, because these visits were always a little formal. There was never a great deal of warmth and I think my mother found it difficult to express it, partly in Karen's case due to her poor English, but generally because it just wasn't in her nature. Also, while she loved to see her grandchildren, she would have us permanently on edge in case they broke any of her countless little trinkets and decorations. We were never relaxed and constantly expecting a calamity.

Equally, I had no close relationship with my sister, because there was a generation between us. I had not really lived with her since she was a small child and she was a very poor communicator. During one of our visits, my mother finally told me about the problems she was having with Gudrun. These had been going on for quite a while, but mother hadn't wanted to alarm me for fear that I would visit even less.

She explained that Gudrun was stealing money from her at times and also taking any drinks she did not lock away. She had even stolen a bottle of whiskey from some of her guests, who as regular customers had come for many years and now threatened to stay away. She had managed to placate them and replaced the stolen goods. It was immediately apparent to me that Gudrun had a drink problem and I was angry that my mother had not told me earlier, before the situation had deteriorated so badly. I remember using the word 'alcoholic' for the first time to my mother, and she did not want to believe it.

I tried to talk to my sister, but of course she didn't want to accept that there even was a problem. She was in denial and she was on a slippery slope from which I was unable to save her. On a later visit, when my mother was again feeling unwell and in bed, I noticed a key around her neck—the key to the little lock-up cupboard, where she now needed to lock away anything that might be of use to Gudrun in aiding her addiction.

As that year was drawing to a close I made the decision to buy Beech Mount House from my mother. I planned to develop it to enable us to earn a living, to let my mother retire, which she really needed to do, and hopefully by being there to get my sister the help she needed. As I had become totally disillusioned by the company in Northern Ireland by that time, I thought it was right to make the decision, which was strongly influenced by the desire to see my mother into a happy retirement with her grandchildren around her and relieved of the daily burdens the large house presented.

In other words, I made an emotional decision, rather than a cool-headed business decision, and when it comes to business one really should not make decisions based on emotions. It would soon prove to be most foolish, though for reasons not entirely foreseeable at the time.

\*\*\*

Early the following year I had paid a visit to my previous general manager in Dublin. I explained the totally unsatisfactory state of affairs in Northern Ireland. He was sympathetic, but not willing to get too involved other than suggesting bringing all these matters to the attention of the resident vice president, whom I duly met. By the end of March the situation became unbearable and I left the position in Northern Ireland.

There was no real opening for me in my previous location. Normally, positions and promotions became available either at the beginning of a year or at the beginning of July, though based on my past success and positions within the company a special position of Home Office Sales Manager was created for me, which was to be a holding position until a suitable Field Executive position would become available. My duties were never quite clear. I did a lot of field investigation work and customer service calls, and I helped to carry out stock checks, but somehow there was no longer a clear goal.

Much of my effort was now taken up with the development of Beech Mount, where I had instructed builders to carry out substantial modifications to the existing old building and to add on a two-storey extension, which would house my family.

When buying the house from my mother, we had divided the property and left her the lovely two-storey natural stone building at one side of the yard and the adjoining small garden area. We would take over the main house and further outbuildings and sheds. My plan was to develop the guest business with the foreign fishermen once more, but, since this was always dependent on the season, to expand the business with a good class country restaurant, which would take some time to develop, but help us to diversify and to build a second string of income.

For this purpose I had the dining room totally renovated; dry lined, tiled, fake oak beams fitted and purchased enough furniture and settings for a country-style restaurant. The kitchen was refurbished with £7,000 worth of Italian commercial kitchen equipment. We had a large gas-tank fitted outside, improved the access and outside as much as possible and generally had the whole place spruced up.

I asked my younger brother Harald to come and join us in our project with his wife, who had helped for years in my father's guesthouse business. Then I also secured the services of Tony, an eccentric though very able and well-known German chef, living locally, who has sadly lost his life in a road accident since. By March the extension with our private quarters was ready and we finally moved from the border. Our Northern Ireland chapter came to a close and there with the arrival of spring a whole new exciting experience seemed to beckon.

# CHAPTER 17

## TRAGEDY

We arrived at Beech Mount to take up residence in our new extension, a shining new annex to the ancient house, which still seemed to fit in well with the other buildings. By the time we arrived my mother had gone to hospital for what we all thought would be another recuperation period, time to get her laboured breathing back into tune and to make her fit for her long awaited retirement.

During one of my early visits alone to the hospital the consultant treating my mother asked to see me. His message was simple and stunning; he did not expect my mother to leave the hospital alive and didn't think she would last much longer. He explained that through the excessive strain on my mother's lungs over a long period, caused by her tuberculosis in wartime, her heart was now also weakened. I was distraught; just now when my mother could finally see the light at the end of the tunnel and an end to her struggle of keeping the guesthouse business afloat single-handed, just when she was looking forward to spending lots of time with her grandchildren, it was all going to be over.

With a heavy heart and with my head reeling with all kinds of thoughts I drove back to Beech Mount almost in a daze. As I rounded the final corner on our lane I saw a scruffy, battered-looking Transit Van and I saw a man in jeans and jumper with a machine pistol leaping from the vehicle and confronting me. The gun bearer identified himself as a policeman, Special Branch, and as he did other officers, some of whom were uniformed and known to me, came through the gate towards me.

The local sergeant was with them and I told him that I had just returned from hospital with the terrible news of my mother's impending death and now found my house swarming with what turned out to be 17 assorted policemen, some of them openly bearing arms. He was very apologetic, but said they were acting on information received; the information being that there was a substantial amount of arms hidden at a German-owned house in the area. Two other houses with German connections were also searched, but nothing was found in any of them.

This was only an unpleasant interlude in the final chapter of my mother's life. Immediately after my conversation with the consultant and on subsequent visits it was extremely difficult to appear cheerful and not to let our distress show through. But we, meaning my brother, his wife and also Karen, had decided that it was best not to spoil what little time remained for her with fear and trepidation. We also decided to contact her only surviving sister, my aunt Gertrude, immediately to give her the opportunity to see my mother once more. Gertrude too was most heartbroken at the news, and decided to come at once. Now of course we had the challenge to make this visit look like a pleasant surprise to help my mother on her quick recovery, rather than a final opportunity to say goodbye.

Throughout this period she looked frail and struggled with her rasping breathing. As expected, Gertrude's visit was a pleasant surprise, but also gave rise to her suspicions and more than once she expressed fear of dying and how much she wanted to live. We had to compose ourselves for each visit and find the right facial expressions and the right words to try to assure her that all would be well.

It was difficult to keep her convinced, because at least one of us now visited daily and as much as she liked the company, it also made her afraid of the seriousness of her condition. On a couple of occasions during these visits she rambled on about conspiracies by the hospital staff to gas her or kill her in some secret collaboration. I spoke with the consultant and he said that this was a side effect of the medication she was being treated with to stabilise her condition; but it was very disconcerting to see her so distressed. Then on her birthday, we all came to visit. She sat up in bed, had even applied some make-up and had her hair washed. She looked surprisingly well and so pleased to see us all; we even shared a small birthday cake with her.

In fact she looked so well and seemed so much more optimistic herself, that I spoke once more with the consultant. He agreed that she had indeed picked up a little and though the long or even medium term prognosis remained the same, maybe, just maybe she might live at least for a few months and be able to leave hospital to be cared for by us in her own surroundings.

I remember us planning to rearrange her bedroom to downstairs to avoid any strain, and discussing other possible measures to make her remaining life as comfortable as possible on our return journey to Beech Mount. However, the next day we received a call from the hospital with news of a serious relapse and severe worsening of my mother's condition. Once more we set off to the hospital and saw my mother briefly; she was not really aware of us and was breathing with some difficulty. We were told that this may last for some time and I decided to go quickly to the hospital shop to get some soft drinks for what looked like a difficult few hours ahead.

By the time I returned a few minutes later my mum had passed away. Had I not gone for that minor errand at that time, I might have been able to spend the last moments with her, but maybe it is better that I was spared that final ordeal.

They say you never miss your mother until she's gone, and it is true. We never had an easy relationship, but she was never a bad mother, just not easily able to express her feelings to us. So often I have wished over the years that I had been able to get closer to her and make our relationship better and stronger, and just when the foundation stones for that were laid with our decision to live side by side, death intervened and robbed us of the opportunity.

My mother did not have an easy life; a childhood in the years of the great depression, her teenage years in war, which also robbed her of her health, leaving her with chronic illness throughout her adult life, a husband who foolishly made her live in a country in which she never felt truly at home. She was a stranger with limited use of the language and few real friends and, in her final years, she had to witness her beloved daughter succumbing to an addiction.

For the first time I had to arrange a funeral and considering her status, it was amazing how many people joined the cortege as it slowly made its way from the chapel to the graveyard. She became the first member of our family to be buried in Irish soil, though it wouldn't be too long before the family grave would be opened again. Emotionally I felt drained by the unexpected death of my mother, and the still to be determined consequences this would also have in relation to my sister and on my business plans.

\*\*\*

Stephanie and Philip had been a great help throughout the funeral, proving their great friendship to us, even though by now we were living quite far apart and our meetings had become very infrequent. It was some time after that when they arrived for a visit at Beech Mount looking somewhat serious. Stephanie had heard from somewhere about my trysts and had told Philip, and both were angry that I had done something to hurt their friend, Karen. The chickens were coming home to roost, so to speak.

I obviously felt that I had let them down too. Needless to say, it was a most difficult and unpleasant time and I unreservedly had to apologise to them for the breach of trust between best friends, and for the awkwardness that it would cause. We fell out over it for a while, but eventually managed to repair our friendship.

With Karen it was of course more difficult and not as straightforward as she saw it. Our marriage was on the line. The following weeks were often difficult, but we had come through a lot in the past, shared many happy memories and three children, who needed us both and whom we loved and, little by little, things settled down again. At any rate we were also most preoccupied with our now uncertain business future. When I say things settled down again, that is only in as far as was possible in our complicated and unusual relationship.

It is very, very difficult and now also very painful for me to try to explain the rationale behind this behaviour, but for me, craving attention for the woman within, if I was allowed release and express my feminine side, I was willing to let Karen live her own life.

If there was blame to be apportioned it would have to be to me or to the condition I wrestled with. Karen could reasonably argue that she had not bargained to be married to a man who felt like a woman and that therefore she was entitled to see our marriage as not exactly sanctified. I felt worried that she might meet somebody else.

She felt that I was bringing another person into our relationship, i.e. my inner female self. How could I seriously defend my rights as a husband when I didn't want to feel like a husband anyway?

How could I object to another man in Karen's life when I was bringing another woman into mine? It didn't matter that the other woman was me.

\*\*\*

Following my mother's death the situation with my sister deteriorated and we had little control over her behaviour, though it affected all of us. On the one hand she was of course deeply upset by her mother's death and maybe there were a lot of guilty feelings as well, as she must have known that her drinking and lack of co-operation had not helped my mother's already declining health. In a letter to our aunt in Germany she wrote, 'Had I known what would happen I would have been a better daughter.'

Gudrun found it quite unbearable to visit her mother's grave.

The truth is, though she initially continued to live in my mother's old bedroom, with Harald and his wife and their son utilising the larger bedroom, and all of them sharing the rest of the house, there was friction all the time. We continued to live across the yard in our newly-built extension; all of us had very little communication with Gudrun. She would usually stay in bed till all hours, eat something, then disappear often until late at night, when at times she would come home drunk and wake up those of us who had tried to do a day's work. She was just drifting, doing nothing useful and seeming to have few aspirations.

Of course we tried to talk to her, tried to point her in the direction of possible jobs, but she was often sullen or would make a half-hearted promise to improve and to find work, which just didn't happen. She had little confidence, no experience and without drink she was a poor communicator.

She also had to spend a few days in hospital as she suffered periodically from asthma attacks. At least there she got to know a pleasant boy, Gunther, though he too had his own problems with epilepsy. Gunther was good for her and I think he quite loved Gudrun, but she did not feel the same. At least for a while it seemed he might be able to steer her into clearer waters, but later he took a job in England.

It was more difficult for everyone to get along, as Gudrun would do next to nothing to help keep the place clean. On a couple of occasions she brought noisy drinking buddies back with her and they would create a foulmouthed racket. We had all had enough; we had all our young children to consider. We sat down with Gudrun and gave her an ultimatum to either abide by a few rules or to find a flat in town.

So in the end, she moved to town, initially into a dingy room in an end of terrace cottage, though she later found quite a decent flat overlooking the main street. Most of the time she lived on her welfare payments though by the end of 1988 she got a few weeks' work in a meat factory.

\*\*\*

After a while though, Gudrun once more came to live with us at Beech Mount. At the same time we had Karen's sister and her two children stay with us as they were in between houses, having sold theirs but not yet able to take possession of their new one.

Throughout this time I had to wrestle with the inheritance problem created by my mother's unexpected death. We had divided the titles of the overall property and now her house with her part of the plot was part of her estate, to which all children were entitled in equal parts. My brother Anthony, then living abroad, informed us that he relinquished his share and therefore the remaining estate was to be divided evenly between my brother Harald, my sister Gudrun and myself. The house was valued at £25,000; the problem was none of us was in a position to buy out the other's shares.

Nobody would be that interested to live in a house sitting like an island on another property, nor would it be a pleasing prospect to have strangers in our midst.

The death of my mother had by now shown me that my decision to buy and run Beech Mount House had been foolish. Now that the main reason for it—to enable my mother to live in happy retirement among family—was no longer possible, my whole idea was losing its appeal rapidly.

Moreover, the early running of the business had not gone according to plan. While one or two weekend nights showed potential and, on one long weekend when the house was full with Swiss guests, we even earned decent money, there were too many nights when we sat around waiting for just two or three guests. The fact was that while those who came loved it and some paid repeat visits, we were well off the beaten track and it would take quite a long spell to get people to know where we were and how to find us. We erected some signs at vital junctions, but we needed more investment in improving the lane to the house and more money for advertising. By now my resources were depleted, all my savings had by now been swallowed up by this venture, and the expected income was not yet materialising.

Soon I found myself back working for another sales company, just to supplement my income. But the set-up with a sales-based company was very different from the business I had been used to. First of all I had to commute a long distance daily on an unpleasant bumpy country road and then I found out that the product was sold through contacts, which are normally friends and acquaintances initially and then spreading out from there through referrals to their friends and relatives. If you have few friends and acquaintances as I did, especially outside the business, it is a sticky wicket. Apart from that, I had never envisaged to be back in sales ever again; the enthusiasm just wasn't there any more. In the meantime, while I was back out there trying to sell till all hours in the evening, Tony, our chef, who expected at least some wages from me, might be sitting there with no one to serve on a quiet day.

So it was one summer evening when I returned tired and irritable and saw that nothing was doing in the restaurant, except for being guaranteed a nice meal, when I decided enough was enough and I made up my mind to sell the whole place again.

We soon placed our property with two local agents, but initially there was no local interest at all. For everyone it was too big and too far out. I then used some contacts overseas and at one time there was a real possibility of selling to a Swiss buyer. It would have meant achieving the asking price and knowing that the buyer would have developed the place in line with my thinking. Sadly, in the end, this party pulled out.

Then, finally there was some local interest. An older couple living with family in a small property nearby had successfully sold two adjoining properties which they owned in London. With the astronomical house prices there, they were now in a position to buy Beech Mount House.

After some re-negotiating on the price, a sale was eventually agreed and we also agreed to sell much of the furniture and fittings. We also agreed to rent the stone house from the new owners of Beech Mount for the time it would take us to build a new house in the vicinity. Nail-biting weeks passed after the deposit had been made before the sale was finally completed. Our dream of a new life with our extended family at Beech Mount had lasted less than two years.

To stay as tenants proved quite difficult once the sale had been completed, both practically and emotionally.

We had now managed to find and buy a beautiful site overlooking a lake at a very reasonable price, from a local elderly farmer, who struggled to water his cattle on the sloping ground. So soon we would be living across the river, not more than a mile from Beech Mount House.

Having the site, we now looked first for a house design which would suit both the site and our aspirations. We found an architect and asked him to draw up plans for us based on another original design of his. It was to be a five-bedroom dormer bungalow to which we later added a substantial double garage with a games room in the loft designed to have room for a full-size snooker table. The refurbished table with its nice original legs, which had once graced the golf club in Malahide, was duly installed.

As soon as the sale of our house had been completed I paid Harald and Gudrun their share of the estimated value of the two-storey stone building, which had been part of my mother's estate. This was just over £8,000 each, no problem in Harald's case, but for Gudrun it proved fatal.

I sat down with Gudrun and tried to explain all the opportunities she now had. £8,000 was still a princely sum for a 21-year-old back then. Together we went to my bank and I introduced her to the manager and made her open a savings and a current account, hoping she would follow my advice and continue to live on her benefits until she managed to find employment and to let her nest egg grow. Gudrun seemed to agree with all I suggested.

By now she had moved into a flat some distance away. She made no attempts to stay in contact with us. Once I called at the flat and had the distinct feeling that someone was there, but nobody answered my knocks on the door.

Once more from letters written by Gudrun to my aunt Gertrude in Germany, I know that she worked for a few weeks in the household of a local company director whose wife was away visiting relatives in England and on 4 December she wrote her last letter to our aunt. Most of the letters are bland, repetitive statements about still looking for work, her asthma, the weather, etc., but they never mention her acute problems with drink. That last letter states that she spent about one month with friends; who they were or where they lived I do not know.

On 28 December 1989, Gudrun was stabbed in her flat. The physical injuries were not severe, but I think emotionally it was one step too far. She managed to recover from her wounds, and I met her again in January 1990. It would be the last day I would see my sister.

On 24 February 1990, a detective I knew well knocked on our door. As soon as I saw him and his expression, I said: 'It's my sister, isn't it? Is she dead?'

Early that morning Gudrun had been found on the floor of a small edge of town cottage, where she had been living for the last few days with a friend. He had been out drinking and when he returned he had first assumed that Gudrun was asleep, but she had taken some drink and a lot of pills and beside her lay a sad suicide note written with wobbly scribbles. She asked for her mother's chain, which she wore around her neck, to be left there, and so it was.

She also wanted her remaining possessions to be given to a suitable charity, but to be honest there wasn't much worth giving.

The bank accounts I had helped her set up less than a year before had a balance of 62 pence left. In a year all Gudrun's money had vanished; I will never know for sure, but can guess at the likely events. She had many friends who were bought with lots of free drink.

Paying her the lump sum for her share of the house had undoubtedly accelerated Gudrun's decline and increasing alcoholism. She had lost her way and felt isolated and unloved; she didn't have the strength to go on.

For the second time the burden of funeral arrangements fell on my shoulders. The first step though was going to the morgue, where I was asked to formally identify Gudrun. When I arrived I was obviously interrupting a post mortem still in progress. Samples in bags were carelessly left in a corner on the tiled floor and a tent-like green sheet was draped over my sister's body. She looked heavy and swollen and her face was severely discoloured, the after-effects of the overdose she had taken. I have never quite managed to get the image out of my mind.

From there Gudrun was to be brought to the small hospital chapel, where a short prayer service would be held. Following this, the cortege would make its 25 mile journey to the graveyard, where Gudrun would find her last resting place beside her mother.

We had to be out of the hospital chapel quite early, but were not to arrive at the graveyard until about 1pm. Both venues had other events booked; a wedding was taking place in the church beside the graveyard at midday.

No matter how slow we would progress, we would have to stop somewhere or arrive too early. First it was with difficulty that the coffin was removed from the tiny chapel through the very narrow aisle. Then we set off on Gudrun's last journey at a snail's pace, but eventually we had to stop at a restaurant and bar, park the hearse discreetly at the edge of the car park, and entertain the mourners with a few sandwiches and drinks, which would normally follow after the funeral.

Eventually we resumed the last leg of the journey, up the hill across the village's main junction, where many people stood, maybe some with genuine sympathy and no doubt others who always came to witness funerals, especially those of the young who died tragically.

It was cold and windy and sleet started falling as the coffin was carried from the hearse to the opened grave. I remember clearly thinking how fitting a finale the inclement and stormy weather was to my sister's short and troubled life. All we could do was stand there stony faced and shivering and somehow get through it.

Of course I have asked myself many times if I could have done more. I did make attempts to get her help. At one time we made an appointment with a psychiatrist in a Dublin hospital. I drove her there and she got follow-on appointments more locally, which she didn't keep.

We helped to get her into a hospital to undergo a detox, but she left again without conclusion. Whatever your best intentions, you cannot change someone else's addictive behaviour—only they can make that decision.

Addiction is a terrifying thing, so easy to get into and so very difficult to get out of, as I now know from having worked with addicts on a daily basis. Often I wonder whether, subconsciously, I took a position working with addicts as atonement for the sister I could not save.

\*\*\*

Meanwhile, I too had to look at changes in my life once more. I couldn't afford to live off the proceeds of the house sale, a large portion of which would be swallowed up by our new house anyway. Having liked my independence I wasn't really interested in going back into regular employment, rather I wanted once more to either run a business myself or to invest in a business in which I could also work at the same time.

I went to the Chamber of Commerce and eventually got in touch with a small company run by a lady, producing a range of interesting wool and health products in a small incubation unit. I met the woman and her business partner, a Northern Ireland-based insurance broker. They convinced me that their company was going to go places, but needed investment to expand to a really viable level. I liked the pair of them, though I should by now have been far more reticent after the Beech Mount fiasco to place too much emphasis on liking people or making business decisions without sound financial examinations.

The money I brought into the company enabled us to move into a larger unit and I received a monthly wage, which was often supplemented by my savings to pay my regular bills. The products looked good, but they were not cheap and never quite found the response they deserved.

There were too many factors working against us. Even though I went to an exhibition in Atlanta to progress our sales in the US market, it never quite took off. Margins were always tight and you were at the mercy of fluctuating exchange rates.

Had I anticipated the problems from the beginning, I might well have thought differently about the venture, but I didn't and the experience left me financially drained of all my savings. I remain in touch with these previous business partners from time to time and I have admired their optimism and belief over the years that somehow, sometime, the big breakthrough will come and I might even see some of my money back. Hindsight is a wonderful thing; the truth is I have not been too clever when it comes to investments.

Our new house progressed slowly; each stage recorded by me with my video recorder, with ever more frustrated voiceovers. The workers hated to see me coming with my camera.

Eventually as rooms were ready enough for painting I would spend long evenings after a hard day's work, often to then find in daylight, that yet another coat of paint would be required. It was mind-numbingly cold work as there was no heating and it was late winter. At long last, around Easter of that year, we were able to move into our new house and hoped to open a new and better chapter after the trials and tribulations of the past three years.

# Chapter 18

## The 90s

The new decade beckoned with promise; we were at last in our new house and I spent a considerable amount of my spare time developing our property. The garden took up an immense amount of time, with lawn mowing and weeding becoming the bane of my life, but I was proud of the improvements from season to season and almost everything I planted seemed to prosper even though the soil was mostly heavy, sticky red clay.

On a warm summer's day it could be Heaven, with the children playing outside and a dog we'd acquired flying excitedly around the house like an animal possessed, his ears flapping and little stub-tail wagging with excitement.

Sitting here now in my concrete tower, it is difficult to conjure up the images of the quiet rural setting that was our home, and it grieves me to have lost it.

Shortly after the happy event of the girls' first communion we were reminded of how precarious life can be. One day Clare was suddenly feeling quite unwell and seemed to get progressively worse. She complained of headaches and appeared to be sensitive to bright daylight. Karen didn't wait long with her suspicions, but took her quickly to our local family doctor, who was excellent with children. He suspected meningitis and asked Karen to take Clare straight away to the hospital as fast as she could, and keep her as still as possible. It must have been a frightening journey with the child wrapped up in a blanket and Karen wrapped up in her worrying thoughts.

Clare did indeed have meningitis and only for the fast diagnosis and admittance to hospital, the outcome could have been horrendous. As it was, we were terrified because the doctors would not discount serious consequences and only said that the next 24 hours would be critical. We were distraught with anxiety and worry and could hardly bear to watch our child suffer so much, not knowing whether there would be any lasting effects from this dreadful illness. But our fervent prayers were answered and Clare made a full recovery.

While we were happy with the steady development of our property, I could not be satisfied with the development of the business into which I had invested so much of my hopes and my savings. A lot of the time I was helping out getting export orders to Germany or the US ready for despatch on time and it was a very hands-on job. In Ireland the market was difficult and limited for the range of health products we offered. A couple of items were added to our product line, more targeted at gift shops, and I made some trips around the country to develop this business, but the orders would generally be small and repeat business slow. Where we succeeded to get lower cost items into chain stores, the margins were too low for our simple methods of production.

In the summer I started looking for new employment and while researching possible businesses of interest, I came across a German-owned factory. I found out the name of the Managing Director and contacted him by phone. He asked me to post my CV, but rather than just posting it, I dropped it in personally, stating casually that I had just been in the area and maybe I could just say hello to the MD. My plan worked, and we had a few words on the corridor where he promised me an in-depth interview. It eventually led to my employment and another chapter in my sales career. Once more I was to become the successful businessman, Paul Grieg, and once more my inner female self started screaming to be let out.

The company, which employs around 40 people in Ireland, is part of a much larger, family owned company with its main factory and headquarters on the continent. Nowadays the company has manufacturing subsidiary ventures in a number of countries, especially in Eastern Europe.

Initially I was given the task of developing the sales of our products in the Irish home market, but soon I was looking abroad to help develop the export sales. With the help of a small team of colleagues reporting to me in places like Belgium, Slovenia and of course the UK, and also the help of a very successful distributor in Poland, the business developed over the next few years, though never quite in line with high expectations.

As the export business developed, so my travelling increased too. There were stretches when I was away every second week with very demanding schedules. Apart from my regular visits to the UK and occasional visits to Belgium, most of my trips took me to Eastern Europe in the end.

I soon found myself on trips that would take detailed research and planning and then endless hours behind the wheel in places like the Czech Republic or Slovakia, Hungary, Poland and the newly independent states emerging from the disintegrated former Yugoslavia.

It was a difficult, often tiring and most competitive business, but also very rewarding. It gave me the opportunity to see many new places; occasionally I would stay over for an extra night to see cities like Salzburg, Budapest, Prague, Bratislava and Krakow, where I would enthusiastically try the local cuisine. It also gave me other opportunities.

Though it is not easy to write about these events now, in the interest of accuracy and honesty, I must also confess to having tried more than just the local cuisine from time to time. The first such occasion was unintended. It was during an annual exhibition in Poznan, in northern Poland, when at the end of the long day I went into my hotel's bar and sat at the counter to enjoy a quiet drink. There were few people there; a few, mostly girls, were dancing on a small dance floor and I was watching without any intention to dance.

I noticed quite a good-looking blonde girl smiling over to me occasionally, but didn't think much of it, though of course I smiled back. Eventually she came over to me and persuaded me to dance with her and her friends. When the dance was finished, she sat beside me, I bought her a drink, and we made small talk. It was a few drinks and dances later when she disclosed to me that she was a working girl and asked if I would like to spend some time with her. I was surprised, because she looked very normal in a nice sort of way. By now I had had a nice chat with her, got to know her a little and liked her, and so I said yes.

It is not easy to explain the reasons and motivations, except to say that I could ask this prostitute to take the more dominant role and to allow me to be as submissive as I wanted, without fear of complicating or subverting our relationship. I could therefore let my mind imagine myself as a woman as much as I wanted.

During another Poland trip I met another attractive girl in a hotel in Krakow, though this time I was wiser and knew that she was there to look for clients. With this girl I struck up a real friendship and saw her on a number of occasions. It transpired that she was fascinated by anything to do with transsexuality and wanted to know everything about it. With her I could be as female as I wanted to be, and be treated as such, and it was genuine, because Bozena never looked for payment after the first time.

I would dress as Paula, and she would give me an honest critique on my make-up and clothes and treat me like a woman in bed.

This was the essence of the confusion for me; I wanted to be treated sexually as female and yet had to use my male sex drive to accomplish it, and would always feel embarrassed at the end about my male sex organs, which exposed the lie that was my inner emotions. It is very difficult to explain these inner conflicts, which any transperson has to deal with, and of course, it is also difficult to admit to these incidents in the past. Even though these liaisons helped me to realise my inner self and be as near to what I wanted to be as I had ever been, and make more sense of who I was, or rather of who I should have been, I am not proud of them either.

Now as a woman speaking about prostitution is quite difficult for me, though my motives even then were quite different from an average male seeking such services. I just wanted to be with someone where presenting myself as female would not be problem. Indeed while such a situation may have been unusual for the girl in question, she would quickly realise that at least it would not present any likelihood of danger or aggression towards her and fear of violence and abusive clients is always at the back of the mind of any prostitute.

While there are a few high class hookers, who have made a conscious decision to sell their bodies in return for the considerable earnings they can generate, fact is that the vast majority of women involved in the sex industry are there, trapped as a result of poverty, lack of normal employment opportunity, addiction, controlled and even enslaved by pimps, who take the lion's share of their earnings, with the women often leading quite horrendous lives with fear of violence at any time, HIV/Aids and other sexually transmitted diseases another constant real danger.

For anyone who has ever travelled from the German city of Dresden south to Teplice in the Czech Republic cannot fail to notice what must be one of the biggest open air brothels. Here girls used to line the main route for miles, day and night, many of them Roma, who are already discriminated against in their homelands.

One day I was with my colleague driving near the outskirts of Novi Sad in the northern Serbian region of Vojvodina, the one area in the former Yugoslavia where its rich ethnic mix of people; Serbs, Hungarians, even a strong German speaking community, had lived side by side relatively untroubled. He pointed out a large complex, explaining that it was a famous clinic where people went for sex-change operations—suddenly my ears pricked up and I wanted to know everything about the place, but as always I managed to hide my feelings and made no more than passing comments, trying to display no real interest whatsoever.

Any of these trips when I was accompanied by a colleague were a potential minefield, especially in this region where we crossed borders frequently. I had made a decision to abstain from carrying anything that might cause embarrassment to either myself or to a colleague, but as these frequent trips offered me at least some outlet for my female self, I found it hard to obey my own rules.

So it was one day when we were about to leave Serbia and re-enter Croatia, a border between two implacable enemies and therefore strictly controlled, that we were stopped by a Serbian border guard or customs officer and he asked my colleague to open the boot to inspect his luggage. My heart started to race, but I stayed where I was hoping the uniformed officer would be satisfied with checking my colleague's bags. Some Serbian was spoken and my colleague said that the guard wanted to see my bags as well. Luckily my colleague had walked around to the front of the car as I got out and opened my bags in the boot of the car.

The officer dug around a bit in my bags and then I saw him half lifting my beautiful auburn wig. There was a moment of pure drama—time stood still; I could literally hear him thinking, but he said nothing, replaced the wig, said okay, and that we could go. He must have worked out in those few moments that there was something unusual about me. He could have destroyed me there and then, but for whatever reason he relented.

I tried to control my palpitations and to look cool and innocent, but I swore to myself not to put myself into such a fraught position again and silently I praised the Serbian border guard for his tolerance.

On another of my frequent trips to that war-torn region, I very nearly came to the end of the line. Early one morning my colleague was driving the company Ford Mondeo. We were on our way from Karlovac in northern Croatia towards the island of Krk for a first time visit to a potential new customer on the Dalmatian coast. Normally our trips would take us in the opposite direction of eastern Croatia, where most of the country's industry is based.

It was early in the day, a damp misty morning, and we were on a twisty stretch of road with a poor road surface, just entering a long right hand bend, at a spot where the road ran along a hill side, supported on the right by a two-metre high wall, beneath which the hill sloped steeply towards some farm buildings far below. I did not think that my colleague was going particularly fast, but suddenly we were sliding and before we had time to think we were airborne, flying off the road, unprotected by any crash barriers, catapulting from the supporting wall.

First we clipped a tree in mid-air on the left side and then we hit the ground hard, the vehicle rolled over once, lifted off and rolled over again, coming to rest eventually on its roof just a couple of yards from the edge of a solid stone outhouse.

This can't have taken very long, but it was one of those strange seminal moments where time seems to stand still and your whole life flashes in front of your eyes. After we hit the ground the first time, I was sure we were going to die; I just closed my eyes and waited for the end, but eventually the car came to rest upside down, with us hanging in our seat belts. My colleague was covered with the by now deflated driver's airbag and was crawling out, shouting all the time at me to see if I was alright and to get out. I could smell petrol and was terrified in case the car would suddenly burst into flames. The door would not open, and it was a struggle to get the seat belt off, but eventually I managed to crawl through the shattered window and stood up gingerly once outside.

We both stood, looking at the total wreckage of the car, bashed from every side, and we were utterly amazed that we still stood, that we were still alive and carried no more than some bleeding, superficial cuts and some bruising.

An ambulance was called and we went back for x-rays and examination in Karlovac hospital, but there really was no serious damage. It was a little difficult for me, as we were standing close together and I wondered if my colleague would notice my now totally hairless body; if he did, he never said, but it was another time when my other side could have been revealed. We had been extremely fortunate; this literally could have been the end of the road for both of us.

\*\*\*

My boss did give me a lot of independence in carrying out my work and I think I earned his respect for my efforts and he knew that I could be trusted to work independently.

When I was in Ireland, I would work from my office, following up with offers to companies visited previously and to plan the next trip ahead, arranging meetings with owners or purchasers at companies to be visited, checking on distances between calls, to pack as much into each trip as possible. There were trip reports to be written and monthly sales reports which would be presented at our monthly sales meetings.

Against this background of work, family life continued and my family was used to my regular absences due to my often hectic travel schedules, but it was this hectic schedule that permitted me to engage in my secret life.

It was by now quite usual for me to carry clothes for both genders on my many trips, which allowed me to live at least part of my life in female role. When in the UK, I also arranged my trips in such a way that I would stay over at least one night in London, where I would arrive as a man and a couple of hours later re-emerge as a woman, to go out for a meal or a few drinks to another nearby hotel, which specifically serves the TS community. By now I had gained enough confidence and expertise to be seen in public as a woman, and to know where to go, and London at any rate is such a cosmopolitan place that you might say anything goes and hardly anyone will take notice.

I also stayed over in Manchester from time to time, which gave me the chance to further interact with the transsexual community. The city's famous 'Village' area had a lot of places that were safe to go to, and it wasn't difficult to locate a couple of venues where transpeople met.

The trips let me live out my secret life, while my children were at home and knew nothing about what I was doing. It was the ultimate deception to them. By this stage, however, Karen was well aware that I packed extra clothes and went out in female mode in the UK.

I soon found out from frequent business trips that Wednesday was the favoured night, where people would gather at one venue, and where changing facilities enabled those who needed them to get ready for a night out.

Later, small groups could venture out with friends, taking in a meal at one of the Village restaurants or in nearby Chinatown, or could maybe go for a pub-crawl through the many colourful Village bars, often ending up on the tiny dancefloor in Napoleon's Nightclub.

There was a small hotel, which had rooms in a nearby annex and was well within my company's budget, so I could arrive in after a day's work, check in, get ready for a night out, dressed fully as a woman, then get up in the morning, a little tired but ready to go back into 'normal' mode. Over breakfast I would have to carefully check that there weren't any remnants of nail varnish or mascara on me, which could trip me up in the working day ahead. While I hated having to revert back to living the lie I increasingly felt I was living, the nights out where I could meet others like me were such a relief, allowing my inner self the free expression I needed.

My heart had been in my mouth the first time I stepped out into Manchester's famous Canal Street, all dressed up and rearing to go, but it quickly became routine as my experience grew. At any rate, in the Village, anything goes, and those who are part of the Lesbian, Gay, Bi and Transsexual community certainly weren't going to be fazed. While you might have to endure the occasional stares from the sight-seers, the Village tourists, you could at least feel comfortable in the area.

I would always return home to my family as the loving husband and father, never mentioning what I had done. I was away on business, as far as anybody knew, and that is the way it stayed.

Nowadays, I keep almost no ties with the wider trans-community, as in my opinion it only hinders assimilation into the mainstream community, but in those early days of my journey of self-discovery it was good to have others I could talk to for support.

I became a member of the Inner Enigma support group for transsexuals, which meets once a month and offers excellent support to people who are often faced with multiple challenges from families, from friends, or at work, and are at risk from prejudice in the wider community.

I have kept up friendships with a couple of transwomen of a similar age, but it is a sad fact that if you socialise with other transpeople, the chance of being hassled, or being 'read' grows disproportionately.

I would also use my stay-overs in London to finally get the expert counselling I probably should have had years earlier. I would see some London customers for my company, then in the early evening, get into my hotel, have a quick shower, get dressed, apply make-up and just make it in time to walk up to my counselling psychiatrist. I would always dress impeccably as a woman, though I was still quite nervous at times in the busy street.

By now things had progressed at home to a stage where Karen had accepted me for what I was and was giving me good advice on what was good on me and what was not, and even letting me have some of her outfits, if they would fit me, though I don't believe she could have imagined the extent of it, or what the future held. She knew that I was getting counselling with a psychiatrist, who almost every transsexual in the UK would have heard of, and who specialised in the field of Gender Dysphoria.

I would also travel to Baker Street to have time with my other psychologist counsellor, whose opinion I valued greatly, as she herself had travelled an even more difficult and similar journey in the 1970s.

\*\*\*

To any outsider looking in we must have seemed almost the perfect family in the 1990s. We lived in a beautiful home in lovely surroundings, we could afford nice holidays and to socialise, we were a two-car family, all our children were succeeding with their education, we were blessed with good health, and all of this was sustained by my secure position within a large international company.

The only way seemed up and yet I was in ever increasing turmoil. My internal conflicts were hidden so well from everyone but they were threatening to tear me and our secure lives apart. I, the typical Libran, who always hated conflict, who would always try to resolve situations, to make peace, to restore harmony, could not find a way to resolve my most important inner conflict, the conflict between the sham 'man' everyone thought they knew, and the woman I needed to be.

My counselling sessions in London continued and I finally found myself fully admitting what I was. I had known for quite a while, and had always suspected something, but to finally acknowledge and come to terms with it was the breakthrough I needed. It did also mean, however, that there was no turning back.

\*\*\*

By the end of the 1990s I had had enough counselling to know that I could not continue to live a double life based on a lie; I was the lie and I needed to be the truth if I wanted to find any inner peace at all, even if that truth would rock my family to its foundations. I did not choose the condition described as Gender Identity Disorder, but now I faced a choice, a choice of deprivations—either I would be deprived of the company of those I loved most; family and friends, or I would be deprived of my own true identity.

# PART 3

# NO MAN'S LAND

# CHAPTER 19

## TRANSITION

'Transition' is a much-used expression among the transgender community, but what does transition mean? It implies having left one place, but not yet having arrived at the final destination. Then again one can be in a state of either mental or physical transition. For example, any teenager can be described as a person in transition, having left childhood, but not yet quite having reached adulthood. Transition means to be in transit, to be in flux, to be neither here nor there.

For a transgendered human, transition usually means all of the above. Often there is a move to a new location to attempt a fresh start, there is then the long period of mental and physical transition, with the help of chemical changes induced through a contra-hormone regime. Then there is hard work to actually learn to live according to the new gender role and to unlearn the habits of the unwanted gender, which have unwillingly and unwittingly been ingrained for years.

For transsexuals, transition is a frightening roller-coaster ride of emotions; relief at having arrived at a decision, fear of failure, moments of euphoria, self-doubt, panic attacks, hope of finally being set free from the bonds of an unloved and unwanted body, expectation and humiliation. For us, transition more often than not means the loss of family and friends, loss of employment and difficulty with new employment opportunities. Every day can be a challenge and even relatively minor incidents can spark bouts of depression or a crisis of confidence. It is no surprise that even in these supposedly more enlightened days the rate of attrition is high and the average life-span of transsexuals is not what it could be, and that is not due to the risks of surgery.

At a most critical phase in a transperson's life, when that huge decision has been made to live true to oneself, much of the past life has to be cast adrift. Family, friends and colleagues may distance themselves progressively or even abruptly. At a time when support is most needed it may be hardest to get, and so for many it is a departure which does not lead to a fulfilling new life, but to an early grave. Suicide rates among the trans-community remain high and many of those occur during the period of transition, where rejection and loneliness can break the strongest spirit.

It is difficult, usually, to put an exact time span to such a transition, though medical experts have tried to impose time limits on transition by stipulating that prior to approval for surgery or even hormone therapy, a transsexual has to live in the role of the 'chosen' gender for a set period of time. At the time of writing some clinicians are talking about increasing this period of the so-called 'Real Life Test' to three years. This period is not much of a life for those having to live it, but then how would the experts know?

If I sound a little cynical, I am no different than most transsexuals who seek help from the medical establishment. If one is forced to rely on the public health service, one is not spoilt for choice. Waiting times can be long and treatment by professionals is more often than not uncaring and diffident, and the level of understanding of the transsexual condition remains low.

If one has the funds to go the private route there are any amount of people willing to relieve the unwary of those funds. In my case everything was funded privately, because having made the most difficult decision of my life I could not face years on a waiting list, nor possibly being treated by second-rate surgeons with little empathy. It may be unfair to criticise the UK and Irish national health services as they do valiant work in many areas, but their reputation in treating transsexuals is by and large not good. It is not surprising really.

There are too few of us to warrant the funding that is required to set up a strong regional network of gender clinics and the funding to do serious consistent clinical research into the causes of transsexuality, which may lead to both better treatment and increasing knowledge among the general public. Knowledge removes fear and without fear there would be less prejudice.

Having listened to the experiences of others and learning from my own experience, I am happy to have chosen my surgeons elsewhere. Of course it also has to be said that in Ireland any gender related surgery is impossible or certainly was impossible at the time I needed it. There are very few specialist surgeons operating in this highly specialised field.

The beginning of transition for a transsexual can be defined as the moment one has come to the conclusion, after a period of in-depth counselling and study of the subject, and by relating to others in a similar position, that one is indeed transsexual.

When I was looking for advice I was lucky to be initially counselled by someone not only with great counselling experience in this field, but someone who herself had walked the hard road through transition at a time when this was still so much harder than it is today. In my opinion, in the final analysis, only those who have themselves undertaken this journey can truly understand all the feelings and implications of Gender Dysphoria.

If I had hoped initially for someone to tell me that I either was or was not transsexual, I was quickly disabused of that notion. It was made clear to me that I would get as much time as I wanted to discuss my feelings and I was given the opportunity to study various books on the subject and told to meet with as many others in a similar position to help me come to a conclusion of where I fitted into the gender spectrum.

It may seem like a bit of a cop-out by the counsellors and psychiatrists, covering their butts so to speak in case things go wrong later, but in the final analysis self-diagnosis based on counselling, study and investigation of other cases is the only way based on current medical knowledge.

Over a period of some years my wife had at first reluctantly accepted my cross-dressing as long as it happened without her presence or participation. This had changed to the point where she would help me with advice but for me, it was by no means satisfactory, as I wanted to be fully accepted in my female role.

Apart from Karen, nobody as far as I am aware, ever suspected my female feelings and as common with many male-to-female transsexuals, one would if anything overcompensate with male behaviour.

To hide my personal female clothing and make-up I had fitted a lock to an overhead compartment of our built-in wardrobe in our bedroom, but I guess I should have known that a lock to a teenager is like a red rag to a bull. The locked space proved a magnet for our son and not much of an obstacle either. With some mechanical implement he managed to open this cupboard in our absence and he must have been quite surprised by what he found. While he had managed to breach my privacy, he had been careless and I was almost immediately aware that he had rummaged through my things. Therefore I felt obliged to take him aside and explain the meaning of all this, or at least explain what I then still thought it meant. I expressed my regret that he had violated what was obviously my private space, created especially to protect him and his sisters from issues which would only confuse and upset them, and with which I had not wanted to burden them.

As one can imagine it was a difficult discussion between a father and his only son, who looked up to that father figure and who must suddenly have been seen in a completely different light. As I was still quite unsure about where all this would lead in future, I tried to reassure him by saying that as long as we kept these matters to ourselves, there would be no problems and it should not affect his life in any way.

I spoke to Karen about this and she was quite horrified that our son was now aware of my unusual behaviour. I was able to persuade her sometime later, that I would also tell our girls about this. Karen was not at all sure about this, but I was quite adamant that I should tell them. There were two reasons for this; I feared that they too would be similarly curious to find out what was in the locked cupboard, find out the wrong way, be confused and upset, and so I wanted to pre-empt this and wanted to reassure them that there was nothing to fear. Secondly, I just wanted them to know all of me and, truth be told, I craved their understanding.

I told them that I liked to dress in women's clothing sometimes, but that it didn't change who I was, and that it was not something they had to worry about because it would not affect the family in any way.

This of course changed. I had not known the vast differences between transvestism and transgenderism.

Telling them proved to be a mistake in the long run, because my reassurance given at that time that this was just a hidden part of me which would not develop into anything, get out of hand or threaten our family, though given in good faith by me at that time, based on my own limited understanding of my gender problems would be seen as a breach of promise by my daughters later on.

Things were of course very strained after that, and the family, contrary to what I had wanted, began to unravel after my announcement.

Karen continued to go out with her friends without me, as I was usually not that interested in the local pubs and clubs, being much more of a home bird. On one such occasion Karen met a man and a genuine relationship developed between them, and she fell in love with him.

My initial reaction was to fight this. I felt genuinely hurt and jealous as I sensed that this was something that would upset the delicate balance of our lives. There were also more practical fears. This new friend was living locally and it would only be a matter of time before either our children or our friends or my work colleagues would learn of this developing friendship.

When I first learned of it, we had a big quarrel and I even issued an ultimatum—something like, 'It's either him or me.'

For some days I went through a period of intense self-analysis, trying to understand my own feelings and motives for objecting to this new situation and I came to the conclusion that it was not only the threat of Karen falling in love with someone else, but also the fear of loss of face and respect if this situation became public knowledge.

Within days my feelings changed to resigned acceptance and, more importantly, I felt that my agonising decision had been made for me. I had been set free. Of course, I had also forced the situation with my own irrevocable first steps on the path towards acknowledging the true me.

She had never been at fault. She had married Paul, but Paul had changed, and was becoming someone else. In effect, our marriage truly ended when I began to talk of starting a medically supervised contra-hormone regime and eventually genital re-alignment surgery.

If Karen had indeed a new man in her life, then I would not have to feel guilty about letting myself be free, to live for a future as the woman I was and I needed to be. This in essence was the beginning of my transition. There followed a period of much planning and, optimistically, we still thought that we could stay close and together in some way or form, share our house even, but as events unfolded this quickly proved to be impossible.

We decided to have one more holiday together, one week cruising in the Mediterranean, followed by one week relaxing in Majorca. The cruise was wonderful and we visited the sites of ancient Rome, wandering among the marble ruins on a scorching hot midsummer day. We gazed in awe at the inspiring art of Florence, the Leaning Tower of Pisa, visited the Vatican, toured through the frightening narrow lanes amidst breathtaking scenery in Corsica, marvelled at the opulence of Monaco and enjoyed the street life and architecture of Barcelona.

It was a magical, even romantic week, but there was always the underlying unspoken sadness—we both knew in our hearts that after all the good holidays we had shared over the years, that this was very likely the last one we would spend together.

There was a willingness to enjoy the moment, and to pretend that our separation wasn't imminent, that the future wasn't so uncertain or even a little frightening. We behaved as a normal married couple, and enjoyed loving each other as husband and wife, just as we had done in the past, but there were also glimpses of a possible future.

In Majorca I bought a nice summer dress, which I still like, and we went out one evening, two friends strolling in the last of the evening sun. It felt good and I hoped that it would be possible to share much time like this in future, no longer as husband and wife, but as two very close and loving friends.

In the week following our return from this last magic holiday I went again on a business trip to the UK and once more used the opportunity to have an evening counselling session with my psychiatrist. Needless to say I attended these sessions as Paula.

\*\*\*

That July I took my very first female hormones. This was the start of my medical transition, which would take two more years to complete. My psychiatrist had agreed that I was indeed transsexual and had prescribed the longed-for oestrogen and also the testosterone-inhibiting drugs the previous day.

Though I brought the prescription to the nearest chemist immediately, I held off taking the first dose for one more day for a very poignant reason. The following day was a significant day for me. It was a birthday shared by both my older brother, and my younger sister who had died tragically 10 years earlier. In a way this date would now be Paula's birthday too.

That whole day I felt elated, happy that the decision had been made. This was the first day of the rest of my life, and the rest of my life would soon be lived as Paula. Over the next few weeks my mood swung from elation at the prospect of my new life and the fear of losing too much from my old life.

Ahead of me lay some of the most difficult things I would ever have to do; telling my children, the wider family and closest friends about my hidden true self and risk ridicule and abandonment. First of all my children needed to know what was happening, but I didn't know how best to approach the subject.

I decided to leave books dealing with gender issues lying around in the hope that my daughters, who were still living at home, would notice, maybe have a look at them, and then ask why they were there.

If they ever did look at them, they never let on and in the end I decided to write a letter, which I handed to them myself, asking them to read it and then to talk together to help them through what no doubt would be quite traumatic for them as well. The letter reproduced here was written by me in August of that same year and from here on the heartache caused by my situation spread to those I loved most:

> *Dear Daughters,*
>
> *Please read this letter together and forgive me for writing rather than talking to you. Believe me it is not that I don't want to talk to you or that I am afraid to talk to you, but it is sometimes simply easier to get one's thoughts across in writing. When you have had time to read and think I do want to talk to you, because we are a family and we should be able to work out all our problems together.*
>
> *Whatever you think about me, rest assured that from the day you were born I have loved you dearly and I continue to speak proudly of my daughters whenever the subject of family comes up. Equally I love Stephen and Mum and it is my family that has given me the strength to get through difficult times in the past and I hope I have done well by my family.*
>
> *I have tried to leave books around for you to trip across, to encourage you to investigate and then to question me about them, but that has not worked. The reason for this is either because you really don't want to be bothered or you are too embarrassed or you don't want to confront possible problems.*

But I have found that any problem can be solved when faced and often our problem pales into insignificance compared to the problems of others.

Now I stand at a difficult crossroads, but I know the path I must take, because if I don't I will never know complete happiness and in the end if one cannot love oneself, one will not be able to completely love others.

I have recently told you about my other female side, but this is a struggle that has gone largely unnoticed by even those closest to me for years. Since then I have undergone further specialist counselling and I now know, that I am a transsexual and I will only complete my life's journey happily if I can live as I feel—as a woman.

Let it be clear that I have no regrets about the past, about all our experiences together, shared joys and at times sadness, but I cannot see another future for me but to be who I am. That does not change the core of my being or my feelings for those I love, it simply means to match my physical presence to my inner self. This in itself involves a painful journey and no one undertakes this lightly, but it really is a choice between life or mere existence.

Of course I am aware that this affects the people I love most and I really want to find the right way to lessen the impact particularly for you both and I will listen carefully to what you think and say. Even if you reject me or you preferred if I moved away or even died, I will always love you and I will continue to support you as I have always done.

Please know that this is the most difficult letter I have ever had to write and I beg you to realise how difficult this path is for me. It is not a simple choice; the choice for

*whatever reason is made for us. We do not choose to be*
*born black, white, disabled, female, male—or transsexual.*
*I am who I am and I will always love my children.*

\*\*\*

It was indeed a gut-wrenching, heartbreaking, tearful discussion, which followed. In a way they felt betrayed, because having told them some months earlier about my cross-dressing and how it would not cause any problems, here I was now telling them that I could only see a meaningful life for me as a woman. They asked questions I was not expecting. The saddest for me was my daughter Clare asking, 'Who will give me away when I get married?'

To make matters worse we used the same moment to explain the existence of their mum's new relationship to them. This was another severe blow, because their parents had always seemed to have such a sound and loving relationship and though I did my best to explain that we still felt a lot of love for each other, the end result would still be a break up of our family. After all, Karen had married me as a man, and since she was not a lesbian, we could hardly remain married as I had now taken the decision to spend the rest of my life as a female. I did my best to convince them that there was no animosity between us, but it was still a lot for two teenagers to take in.

These were most painful days and when our son returned from Europe, where he had worked for a year and a half, it was even worse. He took the news so badly that he started to bleed heavily from his nose and we could not stem the flow of blood for a long time. It was all so agonising and the memory of those hard days still frequently moves me to tears.

When I told my older brother Anthony and his wife, who live abroad, they were very understanding, and since then I have visited them and they have visited me, but unfortunately not everybody was so cool about my new circumstances.

A few days after telling my son, I also visited my younger brother, his wife and my nephew. Being the only other member of my family living close by, I had enjoyed a good and close relationship with Harald over the years. We had enjoyed playing snooker together or going fishing from time to time and I really had expected him to be understanding and supportive. Initially when I told him, he was stunned. He tried to accept the situation, but the next day he phoned and asked to see me again.

By now, understanding and empathy had given way to self-preservation. Working in the town and being well known, he was fearful of how all this would reflect on him and his family. This was also more and more the feeling emanating from my own children and indeed Karen. Where before we had considered living in close proximity, maybe even still sharing a house, on one side Karen with her new man and on the other side her very best friend and soul-mate forever, now I was being asked to live my new life if I must, but not in their back yard.

For some reason I had imagined that in the end they would care less what the narrow-minded people in the street would think, but maybe it was indeed wishful thinking. They could see their friends dropping them, looks and taunts following them, and they didn't want to deal with that. My expectations of how this situation would develop had been far too optimistic. I could not be angry with them, but I was sad, because if they could not find the courage to have me living near them, it meant loneliness and exile for me. I had to leave.

There was also the terrible realisation that, apart from banishment, I would again be asked to live a lie. All my life to date had been a lie with regard to my gender identification and at last I had realised it, made the decision to acknowledge it, and almost immediately I was asked not to live in truth or to tell the truth, at least not among the people I knew. If my family had their way I would not have been able to tell anyone at all why I was leaving. In the eyes of my friends and work colleagues, I would have simply disappeared and left everything and everyone behind.

After more discussion we decided in the end which family members and which closest friends could be told, with the expectation that they would not divulge the information further. For this purpose, I engineered a meeting of those of Karen's family members considered trustworthy and you can imagine that, suddenly facing them, who had known me for more than 25 years and having to explain such an impossible situation, was excruciatingly difficult.

I had decided to use the letter I had written to my daughters as the basis for my explanation and I just told them that I had asked them together to announce some very difficult news and that I would ask them most solemnly to promise not to discuss what I was about to disclose to anyone outside the gathered circle.

There were some really worried faces and one of them asked me if I was seriously ill, and it made me think for a moment. Yes, I was announcing Paul's death and yet the essence of him would live on in Paula, the woman so ready to be born at last.

I think it was clear from the seriousness of my tone and demeanour that this was for real and not some practical joke. There was stunned silence at first, when I told them, and you could have cut the air with a knife. If there had been a hole in the ground some of them would probably have gladly disappeared into it.

Here was a bunch of people who thought they had known me for more years than they would care to admit, and yet they hadn't known me at all. Here were people with very straightforward country backgrounds being asked to comprehend something that they just couldn't get their heads around.

It was my father-in-law who finally broke the silence after an agonising wait. He jumped up, gave me a hug, and said that while he could not at all understand what was happening, I had always been a great son-in-law and he could only wish me well for the future. It was really courageous of him and I have always appreciated that moment and the support he later showed.

Others followed suit with polite bewilderment, and everyone was asked not to spread the news beyond the gathered circle, not for my sake, but for the protection of my children.

***

The summer, with its wonderful holiday, was now a quickly fading memory. My future looked more uncertain than ever. Ahead stretched a damp autumn, and dark winter days. It was clear from all discussions that there was no real option for me, at least for now, but to plan to move away. I discussed the financial implications with Karen, because obviously not only would I have to give up my well-paid job, but the prospects of getting worthwhile employment as a middle-aged transwoman would not be brilliant.

Throughout these weeks I studied all kinds of possibilities of self-employment and hoped to make enough with a mail-order and translating business to hopefully support myself and give some financial support to my family as well. Once it had become clear that Paula would not be welcome to stay, I decided to move to the UK, because there at least I had some acquaintances. After some deliberation I chose Manchester in preference to London, because life, especially housing, is a little cheaper in Manchester. It would be closer to my loved ones as the crow flies, and I would be part of a support group for transsexuals located there.

We had by now decided to place our house on the market and worked out plans of how to cope financially with the future. It was my intention to give my notice at work at the end of the year and even though my contract required three months' notice, I was quite sure that I would be able to leave sooner. But as usual even best laid plans don't always work out.

The housing market had been buoyant in Ireland, but just about the time we finally decided to place our property on the market, prices became more static and even started to go backwards. There is at any rate a distinct division in the Irish housing market, with any property in Dublin and surrounding areas selling at far higher prices and more easily than any property in the country. After that people prefer provincial properties in or very close to towns, whereas our very nice five-bedroom dormer bungalow was six miles from the nearest big town, down a narrow country road.

We all loved our house, having built it to our personal specifications years before. It stood on an elevated site overlooking a lake and I had spent endless hours over the years working to develop the garden, but now probably having put too ambitious a value on the house, we did not find an easy buyer as easily as expected. The months dragged on with no sign of getting the house sold and as winter approached it became evident that the house would not be sold that year, as few people buy houses around Christmas.

Throughout this difficult period I had to somehow continue to function in my role as an export sales manager and to pretend that it was business as usual at work. There were still overseas appointments to be made and seen, and meetings to attend, and the strain became progressively worse. Looking back at it all now I was very close to a complete breakdown. In addition to all the stress, I felt both physical and emotional changes kicking in as a result of my ongoing hormone treatment.

In our management meetings I had always been the one willing to stand up and fight. Now I had two occasions during management meetings where I made my points, but where before I might have reacted angrily to statements, I now found myself on the verge of tears.

\*\*\*

Oestrogen works in mysterious ways. Simultaneously within weeks my body was changing, with first my nipples becoming very sensitive and then breasts beginning to develop, and also my bum started to get a little rounder. All of that of course was most welcome, but also very difficult as I had to hide those changes.

One day one of the girls in work noticed with surprise that I had my ear pierced and then with even more surprise that it was indeed both ears. I tried to cover up as best I could with a joke, but I am not sure what she made of it.

By Easter the situation was becoming unbearable. For example, it was quite warm in the offices and everyone was running around in shirtsleeves, but I could no longer take my jacket off for fear of displaying my budding breasts.

Even though the house had still not been sold, we decided together to raise an additional small mortgage on the house, which would help to finance a few months ahead and would enable me to resign from my position and move to England.

I duly handed in my notice to my very surprised managing director at the end of March, with a view to leaving in June. He was not convinced that I was stating the real reasons for leaving, which I had given as bad health, and asked me repeatedly to let him know why I was really planning to leave. In the end I almost broke down and had to ask for a few minutes reprieve in my own office to compose myself. Then I returned and after getting assurances from him that all we discussed would be confidential, I explained what was really happening.

Needless to say, he was dumbfounded, but also quite supportive. He suggested that I could work in a different capacity within the firm, or indeed I could work for the company's English office. This was tempting as I had no job to go to and my future was financially very insecure, but I had to decline the offers, because after all I was leaving to protect my family's privacy and to keep the situation from becoming common knowledge. Had I worked elsewhere for the company, the news would have filtered back within days to the Irish office.

My boss then asked me to reword my resignation in some way, which would prevent undermining the morale of the management team in any way. So I read out my decision to resign for health reasons, which would require treatment in the UK at next morning's management meeting. Again there was much surprise among my fellow managers and then of course also understandable concern, as it appeared to be something very serious. I reassured them that I was not seriously ill and would be fine in time.

The girls in the office then organised a going-away do for me in a local pub and disco. All the time I had to pretend that everything was fine, but inside I was screaming to let them know why I was really leaving. It was horrible, because I knew that a lot of them thought that I was just abandoning my family. Once more it was also physically nerve-wracking, as everyone was remarking that I must be very hot and for God's sake to get my jacket off, which one girl actually tried to remove.

Somehow I got through the evening and said my final farewells with tears in my eyes and I think a lot of the girls sensed that there was more to this than what they knew. So I walked away from my good management position, the status, and the company car that went with it. The price I would have to pay for being transsexual became very real.

These were without doubt the hardest months of my life; emotional turmoil without end, being in the first stages of transition and yet having to hide both my emotional and physical changes. Soon the real transition would begin and so would my life as Paula.

# CHAPTER 20

## EXILE

If these had been the hardest months of my life, July was without doubt the worst in that period. One day I set off in an old Ford Fiesta, salvaged from the scrap yard and restored to roadworthiness.

The night before we had met up with Karl and Jennifer, my friends of many years, to say more goodbyes over an Indian meal. We chose a restaurant where we were not likely to run into anyone who might know us. They had coped well with the news of my impending transition into someone they were not yet sure how to deal with in future. All that day I had been busy packing up the little car with the essentials I would need in my new flat. American Independence Day, 4 July, would prove to be my last ever day in male mode. My independence was now looming—independence yes, freedom no, because I could not go where I wished, as who I was and my independence would be bought at the price of freedom and loneliness.

Then the dreaded morning with its farewells arrived. It was not long after dawn, and thankfully my girls were too sleepy to fully comprehend the moment. I hugged them hard, stifling my tears. This was to be the last day they would see their dad as their dad.

My tears flowed freely as I waved goodbye out of the car window and slowly descended the gravel drive to the small road below. I waved goodbye to Karen, the girl I have loved for more than 30 years and whom I still love; I waved goodbye to my children, my home, my garden and my adopted country of more than three decades.

I tried hard to focus on the road ahead through my tears; I passed the neighbours' houses; all would be asleep and oblivious to what was happening. A multitude of thoughts raced through my head as I reached Dun Laoghaire.

After boarding with the fully loaded little car, I decided to find a place at the front of the ferry, determined to look ahead only, not to look back at Ireland. That would be too painful. As soon as I disembarked I headed for the first available lay-by, where I changed my clothes, stuffed the last remnants of male clothing into a bin and carefully applied my make-up, covering my red eyes as best I could. It was around 2pm on that day when Paula took Paul's life.

As hard as these last months had been, especially the last days and hours, there was a sense of fulfilment in that moment and in spite of all the heartache that had been and all the heartache which was still to come, I accept myself as who I am. My only regret is the huge price people like me have to pay for just being who they are. Needless to say, I never wished to hurt my family.

By late afternoon I arrived at the flat, which would be my new home. I still live there now almost six years later, but I use the term 'home' in a very loose way. It is a place to live, a roof over my head, but I have lost all sense of home and I am not sure if I will ever feel home again. As long as

I, Paula, cannot return openly to all the places I have lived, I will feel exiled and not at home. Maybe when and if that ban is lifted I might accept England as home. Physically I am housed, but emotionally I feel homeless.

Already in May I had been flat searching in this area, while on business in the UK. There were a few acquaintances living locally who helped with addresses of housing associations and property agencies. I looked at the potential to buy, but it soon became evident that my budget would only buy property in run-down areas with a bad reputation, where I, as a newly arrived transwoman, could expect trouble.

Then I looked for rented accommodation. The initial properties offered were again low rent properties in dubious areas with a multitude of boarded up doors and windows— nothing to inspire confidence. But then I was offered a 15th floor flat, close to the housing office. I decided after just one look that it would serve my purposes for the time being. It would take a lot of cleaning and decorating, and I would also have to spend some of my scarce resources to make the place reasonably comfortable.

What swayed me swiftly to accept this flat were the magnificent views offered across the city of Manchester, sweeping up to the hills of the Pennines. I can see the impressive roof of the new City of Manchester Stadium, not built when I arrived, out of one window and across the modern office buildings looms Old Trafford. I can see as far as the Trafford Centre and beyond on good days, and I can see clearly as far as the control tower of Manchester Airport, and dream of the short flight back to Ireland.

Once more I have become a city dweller, but I often miss the garden I nurtured and the peaceful views from my old bedroom window over the still waters of the lake. Now I made myself busy, registered as self-employed, and worked when I could on setting up my mail-order business. Whenever there was work for technical translations I did those. In between, I was busy painting and decorating, buying some furniture, cooking and getting more adept at getting ready each morning. I worked as much as I could, because when I stopped I would start thinking, and if I started thinking, it more often than not ended in tears.

By October the house still had not been sold, but a friend made a generous offer to loan me the money I would need to stay afloat until the sale was made. On 19 October I checked in for a rhinoplasty surgery, or a 'nose job' in a hospital. It would be my only surgical procedure in the UK; it would leave me more than £3,000 poorer and less than satisfied with the result. It probably is a marginally nicer nose but by no means the nose I had expected. But that is surgery for you.

A few days later I received a letter from the courts in Berlin dealing with my name change application, and at last after 18 months I was now legally Paula Grieg. Changing your name is a much more serious step in Germany than in the UK, but it is also the first step towards an application for Gender Change under the German Transsexual Law. Though at the time I looked a mess with multi-coloured swollen eyes and a dribbly nose in plaster, I felt like singing with joy. It was another milestone on the arduous journey to womanhood. Soon I would be able to get a new passport, and post-op I would also be able to get a brand new birth certificate with that wonderful word 'female' on it.

There were other milestones. For example, soon after my arrival I looked out for a suitable church where I could reflect and worship. There was a small Catholic church beside the nearby market, but to me it looked dilapidated and uninviting. Eventually I found a Cathedral just a mile or so from my flat. It was with my heart in my mouth that I went there for the first Sunday mass, totally self-conscious, not at all sure what the congregation would make of me. I asked myself: would I be welcome? Would they notice? Would someone, the priest himself maybe, drop me a quiet word afterwards to say that people like me are not welcome in the church?

It went well; there were a few furtive and quizzical looks and then again maybe they were just my imagination. The people were friendly and encouraging and soon I got to speak to Fr John, the then Dean of the cathedral. One day he saw me in the local shopping centre; he could easily have avoided me, but made a point of coming over and saying hello. I was relieved and touched. Later he asked me to be on the welcoming committee, to stand at the main door of the cathedral before mass begins, welcome everyone, and hand them the parish news bulletin and song sheets.

I was delighted to be asked, but a little fearful. I asked him if some people might have a problem with my welcoming them. Fr John assured me that if they had a problem, it was their problem and not mine. Going to Mass on Sundays became a cornerstone of my life and faith has helped me through the darkest moments of the past years.

In my block of flats there was a small meeting of residents in a community room on Wednesday mornings, for tea or coffee and gossip. Once more I was nervous, but I had decided to face challenges head on. Sooner or later they would talk about me anyway, I reasoned, so I decided it would be sooner. I refused to hide, because as Paula I have been hidden for a lifetime. This approach worked and people by and large have treated me with decency and respect. There were only a few isolated incidents when I was insulted or abused, usually involving young men, early on.

In fact it was one particular day on my regular walk to the shops when, unusually, two incidents happened close together to change my own attitude to my situation. As I left the block compound I noticed a youngish couple walking with a pram. They were looking at me, talking and grinning. Then the woman came over and asked: 'Excuse me, what time is it?' I gave her the time in my best voice but I knew immediately that she was not interested in the time, but only in my voice, to confirm that I was transgendered as they had suspected. I was annoyed at being exposed, and annoyed that the young woman tried to embarrass me. On my return from the shops a young lad on a scooter shouted some verbal abuse, including the word 'tranny'.

I ignored it and carried on walking, but when I finally reached the safety of my flat I was quite distraught at these two incidents in one day. I cried with anger and frustration and a little self-pity. All afternoon I thought about those incidents and why they might have happened. Since then I have talked to other transsexuals about these kinds of incidents and how best to handle them.

The problem is that many transsexuals can only accept seeing themselves totally in the gender they identify with. Sadly, often that is quite unrealistic, because of give-away features such as large hands or feet, a strong brow line or chin or a deep voice. Knowing this, they lack confidence and that lack of confidence more often than not gives them away before any peculiar features do.

No doubt I was like that at the beginning; walking with a drooping head, trying to make myself invisible at times, but I made a decision that day. From that day on I would be proud of who I was and I would not hide anywhere. If I was challenged, I would meet the situation with a smile, tossing back my hair and proceeding with confidence. This has worked very well and because I am so confident now in who I am, I hardly ever have any incidents questioning my gender. On 23 November, I wrote in my diary:

*A month on and things are happening fast. A few days ago I received the official document from Germany confirming that my name according to German law is now Paula Grieg as from 6 November. Earlier in the month the Decree Nisi was read out in court, which means that a long and mostly happy marriage is running through its final chapter. On 18 November, the Decree Absolute will dissolve our official bond, but our bonds will always be there. No legal niceties can take away more than 30 shared years. At the same time I have been informed by the Regional Marriage Tribunal of the Constitution of the Court that they will now deal with the application for an annulment.*

*Today my mind is so restless, because I have booked flights to take me to Thailand for the GRS surgery on 6 December. Already I have told some of my friends about it. It is of course a very final step and not without risks, but I am mostly excited about leaving the transition period and getting closer, hopefully, to a higher level of normality in my life. After my return from Thailand on 20 December, if all goes well, I will go to Ireland and look forward to recuperation among my loved ones. On the one hand I so look forward to spending time there and on the other I am really sad, because I will not be able to carry many gifts this Christmas and it reminds me of hard Christmas times, which I thought I left behind many years ago. Again the price of being a transwoman is acutely felt.*

*There is other gallows humour in my mind also. 6 December is St Nicholas Day and it brings back German childhood memories. While children get their bigger presents on Christmas Day or Christmas Eve from the 'Christkind', on 6 December St Nicholas visited secretly overnight and filled children's stockings with sweet things and nuts. This St Nicholas Day I still hope for sweet things, but as for the nuts ...*

\*\*\*

I still remember collecting the *Decree Absolute* from court later that November. After filling in whatever needed filling in, the lady behind the counter said: 'Well that was easy then, and it's good news,' at which point I grabbed the document, and burst into tears, saying: 'No you don't understand,' and I ran crying from the court. The good woman phoned me later at home and I apologised for my outburst and she apologised for making the well-meant though hurtful remark. For me it formally ended a long and mostly happy union, and I was distraught that day, not happy. It was a vital and necessary step to legalise my life, but it was no occasion for joy.

Around this time I also received a donor card. The liver won't be much use to anyone after the hepatitis I caught in Africa many years ago. There are the practical considerations of possibly helping someone some day with more to live for than I have, but there is also a romantic notion that some day once more the beat of my heart may quicken with the joy of love even if it's not meant to be in my body.

I had chosen Thailand after a lot of research. I wasn't prepared to go to the end of a NHS waiting list, while going private in the UK, or the US, or even Europe, was too expensive. Thailand has cutting edge surgeons with a good reputation and lots of verifiable experience.

The doctor I planned to meet came with very good references, and even though the standards of care were excellent, the overall monetary cost of everything I had done, including electrolysis, etc, was at least £10,000 cheaper overall than it would have been in Europe.

\*\*\*

One day there was a very interesting documentary on television, which followed the lives of three transsexuals up to and through surgery. As the programme progressed I was in floods of tears once more and afterwards I tried to analyse why I cried so much. I cried because of course it reminded me so vividly of all that had happened to me so recently. I cried because I was watching the programme alone. I cried because the three individuals managed to stay in their communities, when I couldn't. I cried for the countless others equally affected but without the money to get the treatments they need. I cried because I suffer from a condition I did not choose but for which I am outcast. I cried because the programme was excellent and if everyone saw it there would be less ignorance and prejudice and more understanding. But few people will have watched, because there are so few of us.

Five months had passed since that sad day when I left family and home behind and now I would leave England for a few weeks to meet the challenges of physical transition, gender realignment surgery, in far away Thailand.

# CHAPTER 21

## THAILAND

On 4 December Becky, a transsexual friend, brought me to Manchester Airport. The check-in went without incident, though I must have felt a little nervous, because at that time my passport was still the old German one with my old male name and a picture that no longer showed a true reflection of me. Inside the passport was a letter from my psychiatrist confirming my transgender status, and also the UK name-change deed poll.

After the change of planes in Istanbul the check-in once more proceeded without incident, apart from a few curious looks. The 11 hour flight to Bangkok lay ahead. As I looked down on the mystical city of Istanbul below, once more memories came flooding back. A few years previously I had visited this fascinating city with Karen, who accompanied me on a business trip. That time we crossed by hired car over one of the two majestic bridges spanning the Bosporus, crossing from Europe into Asia. Now the tall bridge lay below me and once more I was crossing into Asia and preparing to finally cross from my genetic male body to the real me.

Quite exhausted, I arrived in Bangkok and there I was collected, greeted and put at ease by Dr Chettawut's nurses, Tair and Nam. Over the next two weeks they would spend a lot of time with me. About an hour later, after negotiating the bustling streets of Bangkok, we arrived at Dr Chettawut's clinic and introductions were made. We concluded the administrative matters, such as paying for the surgery and filling in consent forms, and then a first examination took place, which was not nice after travelling in the same clothes and make-up for almost 24 hours. The examination was satisfactory and Dr Chettawut was confident that all would be well. He exuded a quiet air of unruffled confidence.

The nurses then invited me to a restaurant for a Thai meal, but the fact that I knew this was my last pre-op meal, and that I would be losing the benefits of it later that evening with the help of enemas, played on my mind. Having finished my green Thai curry, we drove on to the large general hospital, where my surgery was planned for the following day. Again a whole check-in procedure had to be observed, but I noticed immediately how nice all the staff were.

Later that evening, long after Tair and Nam had left, I got my nether regions shaved. Then came the enemas to clean me out. No more food then for the next couple of days. In spite of everything ahead, I was totally calm and looked forward to getting the surgery over with. I managed to fall asleep surprisingly easy.

Then the day had come. It was warm and sunny outside, while inside the air-conditioning was humming. It was such a significant day, but I would not be aware of most of it as it slipped by. I had woken early, because from 6am the nurses were scuttling about.

It was nearly 9am before I got collected on a trolley and I was brought to the next floor and the operating theatre. In the corridor Dr Chettawut met me briefly, held my hand, and gave me a few words of encouragement. Then I was wheeled into the operating theatre. My heart started beating a little quicker. This was it! I was introduced to the anaesthetist, and the friendly face of Nam was also there. All were in their green surgical gowns. I was transferred to the operating table from my trolley, and they were quickly ready to strap me down, but suddenly I realised that I needed to use the toilet one more time. I was brought to the toilet, and on the way back I inadvertently looked through a porthole-like window of an adjoining theatre and saw someone else lying flat on an operating table. I quickly averted my eyes. I was not afraid, but I didn't want to see all the gory details. Once more I was placed on the operating table, more like a narrow bench with two side benches at right angles on which my arms were placed, and then, thank God, I very quickly got my anaesthetic and drifted off immediately.

\*\*\*

When I woke up the first time I was confused and asked what day it was. Nam was there laughing. It was still the same day, but late in the evening. The operation had taken 11 hours. In that time the surgeons had performed three separate procedures; gender re-alignment surgery, a trachea shave, to reduce my Adam's Apple, and breast enhancement surgery, but I was told everything went fine. I felt numb and drowsy and very confined with my bandages strapped around me while lying on my back, as I would be for the next five days. Morphine controlled my pain and I drifted in and out of consciousness for a while. When I woke again I took in my surroundings and tried to make out my body changes. I could see the bumps of my bandaged breasts, but otherwise I couldn't see or feel much of my body. I counted six tubes connected to me—four taking waste from my armpits and groin, one was the IVF line, and one was the catheter.

Many thoughts went through my head, and I thanked God that it was all over. Already I looked forward to getting up and about again.

The next few days were very uncomfortable; I developed some bedsores from lying constantly on my back. For the same reason I slept only fitfully, because usually I never sleep on my back, but on either side, which I couldn't do now. By this time I had adventurously eaten my way through the limited Thai hospital menu. Some things I liked, some I'd much rather have forgotten. I was constantly reminded to drink more water. The nurses were very friendly, but most had very limited English and it was quite funny to watch us trying to communicate. Dr Chettawut and his nurses came to see me every day. Finally after a few days the packing was removed from my vagina, and some of the drains were removed from my body.

Now I was asked to exercise as much as possible to prevent any deep-vein thrombosis from developing. Eventually one evening the catheter was removed and that's when a problem became apparent. It was evening and the night shift was on. I felt I needed to go for a pee, but when I tried nothing came out. Again and again I tried with ever shorter intervals and ever increasing, excruciating pain. I spent most of the night on the toilet, hunched and sweating, and in agony. I kept refusing help because I thought that if I couldn't get through this and pee naturally that night, I never would.

Finally, in the morning, an English-speaking doctor explained that I needed to be reconnected to the catheter and I filled an enormous jar. Dr Chettawut later explained that this sometimes happens—an oversensitive reaction to muscle tranquillisers, leading to temporary paralysis of the muscles controlling the sphincter and urethra. He says this would not be permanent, but could last a few days or even a couple of weeks, but that it could be overcome by use of a mobile catheter.

Initially I was just happy not to be in pain any more, but I did worry about this unexpected problem and its consequences in the days and weeks ahead. Eight days after the surgery I was leaving the hospital with all the nurses saying goodbye and wishing me well. For the next week Dr Chettawut and his nurses would take care of me in my hotel room with frequent visits.

Now I was no longer connected to a permanent catheter, but they inserted a catheter during their visits to allow me to relieve myself. Tair and Nam were wonderful in their care for me, especially Nam who slept in my room so she could help me during the night with my toilet problem. One evening, with the room only faintly lit with the last glows of sun penetrating the curtains, I saw Nam, who thought that I was asleep, quietly kneeling at the end of her bed and offering Buddhist prayers, bowing her head with quiet, dignified rhythms.

She was such a tender, loving natural born carer, not a Thai but an ethnic Lao from the border regions of the two countries. She had left her mother and her husband on their small farm and come to Bangkok to earn extra money for the family.

I was then taught how to dilate my new vagina daily to maintain its depth and also how to massage my breasts vigorously to get the implants to fit in properly and to stay supple.

One evening after Nam had helped me once more with the catheter she decided to go do a little shopping and go to her flat for a couple of hours, to have a shower at home. Shortly after her departure, I felt the urge to go to the toilet. I tried, but again I couldn't pee naturally and I did not know how to use the catheter myself.

Once more I went through ever-increasing, excruciating pain; sweat was trickling off me. I used towels to dry myself and also to muffle my cries of pain. I was close to fainting, but I knew I somehow had to hold out until Nam or Tair returned to me. In my desperation I turned to prayer; I prayed intensely and asked for help with my pain right there in the undignified location of a toilet in a Thai hotel, where I sat crumpled and exhausted on the floor, and then I had a deeply spiritual experience. I could feel an inexplicable presence, calm came over me, and my pain just vanished. I was deeply moved by this experience and was still overawed by it as I heard the knock on the door and the arrival of Tair.

As the day for departure drew near it was becoming obvious that I would still be dependent on the catheter for some more time and the nurses started teaching me how to sterilise the unit, and insert it into my own urethra with the help of a little mirror. At first I was terrified and thought I would never be able to do it, but after a few tries I learned to manage it.

Finally the day of departure arrived. First, I was collected from the hotel and driven once more to Dr Chettawut's clinic for a final check-up and a little rest, before late in the evening they brought me to Bangkok Airport and we had a final meal together there. We said our goodbyes and I was sad, because I had really come to like my two nurses very much.

The check-in went okay and I boarded the aircraft. My hope of finding the flight not fully booked and maybe offering me the opportunity of stretching out on a row of back seats was dashed. I ended up sitting in a forward row surrounded by a number of infants who took it in turns to wail throughout the long flight. Every now and then I nodded off for a little while; in between I got up to stretch my legs, aware of the increased post surgery risks of DVT. My skills with the catheter were now put to the ultimate test. What I had learned to do in a comfortable hotel room with ample space I now had to do in the extreme confinement of an aircraft toilet. It was quite horrendous, and I had to go through this procedure several more times on my way home.

By the time we completed the first flight to Istanbul I was quite exhausted. Then it was time to board the next flight, and suddenly I was asked to step aside, and a supervisor was called. All this happened with other passengers around, arousing curiosity, but I was frankly too exhausted to care. They were not happy with the discrepancy of my passport and my ticket, even though the supporting letter was shown as well. I told them that Turkish Airlines had processed me during three previous check-ins and surely they couldn't now stop me from returning to the UK. They had a prolonged discussion among themselves, but finally I saw the shrugging of shoulders and I was waved through.

I arrived utterly exhausted back at Manchester Airport, but my lift arranged previously with a friend was not there. I just wanted this long and arduous journey to end. I had been through a lot, and I just wanted to be home. I called my friend on my mobile phone, and thankfully she arrived, all apologies, and at last I got back into my flat. But I didn't really have any time to relax.

Only three days after arriving back from Thailand I was flying off to stay with my family in Ireland. So, instead of resting, as I should have been, I had just a few days to get Christmas presents sorted out and to prepare myself for the visit ahead.

\*\*\*

Arriving in Ireland for the first time as Paula should have been a very special occasion for me, but of course I was quite exhausted, anxious and both happy and sad at the same time. Exhaustion was hardly surprising—I was still very much recovering from major surgery and still felt quite weak. And of course I was anxious, as I could not be sure how my children would cope with meeting their new 'second mother'. Still, I was happy at the prospect of meeting my family after such a long and difficult absence. Finally, I was sad, because I would essentially be in hiding, not allowed to be out, and open, and just me. My family had asked that this be the case.

It was a very surreal situation all round, and though everyone made a real effort to behave as normally as possible, everyone must have had different private thoughts.

There was the usual exchange of gifts under the Christmas tree, but this time I had played no part in decorating it; it would maybe have been too strange to try to fit myself back into the old family traditions. Our time together was good, but it was not like Christmases past, and looking realistically at the situation I realised that, unfortunately, it never would be again.

As long as nobody called round to the house, everything was okay. But if there were visitors I was to stay out of sight. Having to hide in my own house felt terribly humiliating but, after all, I had left Ireland in the first place to protect my children, and now was not the time to come out openly, though I dearly wanted to.

My brother came out to visit too. It was all polite enough, but you could sense the uneasiness all the same, and I realised with a terrible sadness that, though we love each other, I felt our relationship was fractured.

I knew my family didn't want me to reveal to the world that I was now Paula, not Paul, and I had agreed to keep it secret so as to protect them, and deep down I just had to accept that this was what they wanted. They had not asked for Paula; but neither had I—she was what was inside of me and I couldn't have gone on without letting her out, releasing her from within. We all just had to get on with things as best we could, though we all knew there would be many challenges ahead.

The most surreal, and now looking back, funniest moment, was when my daughter Sally came unannounced into my room, where I had withdrawn to go through the dilation ritual which is quite essential for any post-op male to female transsexual. Early after surgery it is important to dilate the vagina frequently, to stretch it and prevent loss of width and depth. So you can, if you must, picture me lying on top of the bed, spread-eagled, holding a dilator in place, when suddenly Sally was there. She stood there frozen while I tried to explain that what I was doing was nothing sexual, but rather a medical necessity. I don't know who was more apologetic!

Then belatedly on St Stephen's Day I got the nicest Christmas present of all—suddenly I was able to pee again, and could finally discard the hateful catheter, which I had had to carry and use for two weeks. Never did a woman enjoy a pee more than I did that day.

# CHAPTER 22

## UK

After my return from Thailand I had to take stock of my financial situation and face the fact that in spite of my best efforts, I could not continue with my self-employed status. The mail order business was barely breaking even and the translation work was too infrequent to pay all my regular bills without using savings. I worked out that I would actually be better off on Job Seeker's Allowance, which would then also entitle me to Housing Benefit, than I would be if I carried on as I was.

So, very reluctantly, I presented myself at the nearest Job Centre and registered. I am proud that I have supported not only myself, but also my family throughout almost my entire working life without needing state benefits, but now I was in need. Within a short time my attention was drawn to a possibility to go for assessment with one of the leading world-wide car rental firms, who operate one of their two major European booking centres close to where I live.

I got my first interview and was invited to take part in their assessment day, which I passed with flying colours. I was offered a contract as a booking agent for the European team, which would at least give me the opportunity to use my native language again and also to meet up with other ex-pat Germans living in Manchester. And so, that March, just three months after my major surgery, Paula Grieg was employed.

Compared to what I had been doing previously, this was starting at the very bottom of the pile again, but it was on the other hand a first job for Paula and I had cleared another hurdle. Walking through a busy call-centre for the first time, utterly self-conscious and vulnerable, was like all those first-time experiences; anything but easy. But I had by now got used to facing daily challenges and I knew that the day I started hiding I would be lost.

The successful candidates were invited for two weeks of sales training, where we would learn all the necessary skills of call management and telephone selling in a competitive environment. For me it was in many ways the worst job I could have had, because it would cruelly remind me, on a daily basis, of my predicament. Though I always introduced myself with my proper name, at least a couple of times a day a client would think he had misunderstood based on the tone of my voice and address me as Paul. The other team members became used to hear me saying: 'In spite of my voice, it is Paula!'

Though I have managed to change my voice somewhat through speech therapy and practice, it is one of the most difficult things to change. Surgery offers no more than a 50% success rate and often a worse voice if it fails. Therefore, it has never really tempted me. Generally, people don't notice my voice too much in face-to-face conversations, as they see the whole package with female looks and gestures, whereas on the phone it is only the voice on which the listener can base his or her assumption. Therefore call-centre work can be difficult for transsexuals and their self-esteem.

Still, I had a job and I learned to handle this difficulty too. At least I had a regular income again and the possibility of achieving some bonuses when exceeding the monthly targets of reservations. The training started with unexpectedly informal introductions. There were about eight or nine of us; just one other girl, Sue, who I liked instantly. She had a really husky voice, which I found most comforting.

By way of introduction we were all given some magazines, a blank A1 flip-chart page, some scissors and paper glue with the instruction to cut out meaningful pictures or words with which we could summarise our lives to date and so introduce ourselves to each other. There and then I decided to be honest and open and so remove speculation and doubt. I put my page together, showing among other things a twin-buggy, and some nice houses and cars, and I began my introduction by saying: 'I am Paula Grieg, I have three children, including twins, and no stretch-marks ...'

My introduction was well received and my honesty appreciated by my future colleagues. Having successfully completed the sales training, I was assigned to my first team.

Later I was transferred to a different team and once more I found the people I worked with by and large very nice, though a call-centre environment doesn't lend itself well to building relationships, as you are paid to be on the phone and not to chat to each other.

In early May, after 15 letters and many months, I got the long-awaited letter with good news from the court in Berlin, recognising me legally as female and allowing me to apply for my new birth certificate from the town hall of my native city. I had needed two supporting statements from my surgeon and an expert in the field to go with my application to be legally registered as female, and it had been a long drawn out affair, but at last I was legally a woman. All this had taken a year, but I was elated. At least in legal terms my transition was completed.

This was actually long before a UK or Irish citizen could make the same application. Last year the UK brought in Gender Recognition Certificates, leaving Ireland and Albania as the only countries not allowing transsexuals new birth certificates after a process of evaluation and counselling.

When I received my new certificates and proudly told my father about them, he believed that they were falsified documents, which saddened me, but then he had not taken my news well the first time around either. Whereas my half-sisters and my father's new wife were supportive of me, he had found it all quite incomprehensible. This wasn't surprising, I guess, for a man of his age who grew up under a regime where the likes of me would very likely have been killed along with Jews, gypsies, and other perceived misfits.

Contrary to my father's belief, acquiring my new birth certificate was in effect a thorough legal procedure, at the heart of which lie two detailed expert opinions from experts in the field of Gender Identification, who both counselled me. The document is in effect acknowledging that the brain, rather than the genitals, determine your gender.

\*\*\*

I used my holidays that year to return to Thailand once more, this time for some facial surgery. You could say it was 50% vanity, but also 50% necessity, to give me a more enhanced female appearance. When I returned, both Dr Chettawut and his wife, and the nurses, welcomed me warmly, and the nurses at the General Hospital were delighted to see me again.

For some reason, this time they left me for nearly half an hour on the operating table, before finally the anaesthetist arrived to send me into oblivion. Dr Chettawut had been delayed somewhere; it really isn't nice waiting alone on an operating table, speculating about what it is going to be like to have your face cut up, looking at the cold lights above, and the glinting instruments on nearby tables.

When I came round I looked a real mess, and over the next few days my face was severely swollen. I was covered with a multitude of colours and God knows how many stitches. Though I had thought that I was prepared for this, it was very difficult. I developed a large haematoma along the left side of my lower face and neck; clotted blood under the skin, which looked hideous and eventually had to be punctured to release the blood within.

A friend, who had travelled with me for her own gender-realignment-surgery took a picture, which showed my head like a balloon. I cried in my hotel room, lived on room service, and hid as much as possible. I thought I would never look right again, but of course after a few days the swelling eased progressively. On the last day Dr Chettawut removed the multitude of stitches around my face and neck and around my eyelids and I was able to hide the worst of the discolouration with make-up.

Even by the time of my return to work it was still not possible to hide the bruising completely, but I reassured everyone that I had not been beaten up, and anyway, the difference in appearance was evident. There was no use in hiding the fact that I had had a face-lift, with which I was quite pleased and which certainly enhanced my appearance and made me look both younger and more female.

When a split-shift arrangement was offered at work to employees, there were few takers, but I soon volunteered, as it suited me. I lived close by and as I had now registered in a local gym I could use the four-hour midday break for my regular gym visits. Also this split shift meant that I did not have to work the weekend shifts. On the down side, I now had to get up at 6am to get to work by 8am, because I felt I had to take more care of my appearance than anyone else working there.

***

My first gym visits were another trial of my strength of character. In the early days I felt that quite a few women felt the need to go to the toilet while I was having a shower, maybe to assure themselves that I was indeed all woman, then again it may have been no more than my imagination, fuelled by my insecurities. Now I am training there for three and a half years and I am just accepted as one of the regulars. And not a shy regular either. I am not in the least fazed by being seen naked by other girls, as I am now proud of my body. More than once I have taken my place in the sauna during the times allocated for ladies and told men, who often ignore the time rules, to leave.

My work-outs three times a week have helped me to lose about 6kg in weight and more importantly, have given me fitness and energy, and a sense of well-being. Possibly because of this regular exercise I have managed never to miss a single day at work ever since I started working in the UK more than five years ago.

I decided not to go to Ireland the following Christmas, because of the limited time I would get off from work, but also because I couldn't face the humiliation of having to hide from people again. I felt that I couldn't take a step backwards, which is what it would have been like if I had gone back to Ireland and hidden from everybody but my family.

Christmas therefore loomed as a lonely prospect, but then my dear friend Sonja, another team leader with whom I liked to chat whenever work permitted, sensing my difficulty, invited me to her house, which she had bought recently, for a Christmas dinner. It was a kindness at a critical time; facing my first ever Christmas really alone, a kindness I will never forget. Though we don't see each other often, for me Sonja is my best and closest friend.

As the months passed I did flirt with the idea of trying to progress once more to a team-leader's position, something I had after all done successfully, albeit not in a call-centre environment. Based on my sales results I was selected to a team of key agents, used to monitor and help train others, but the more I looked at what the job involved, the less I liked it. Whereas in my time as a team leader it had all been about one-to-one training, here everything seemed to be computer driven; numbers and statistics in every minute detail, logging even the time taken for a pee. Never did

I feel more like a number than in this environment, but I guess it is necessary and in the nature of call-centre work.

Having dismissed the team leader route as not particularly enticing, there were few other avenues of progression or even varieties of work within the company. Few agents stick this role long-term, because it is simply so repetitive all day long, the same script over and over again. It does get boring, especially for anyone who likes a challenge.

All in all I stayed 20 months with that company and I can say that they were an excellent and fair employer and that I met many nice people there. It was the nature of the work rather than the company that drove me to new ventures in the end. I am glad of the opportunity offered at a critical time and remember fondly many of the people I worked with.

This was a valuable experience for me. I, Paula, had proven that I could succeed in a busy work environment, be accepted and respected by colleagues. I could and would face my fears, whatever my gender problems. My skills were still the same and I was beginning to develop a few new ones as well. I was becoming a whole other person.

# CHAPTER 23

## MOVING ON

One day after Mass at the Roman Catholic Cathedral, which had by now become my regular place of worship, I studied the weekly parish bulletin and noticed that the Cathedral Centre was looking for an additional co-manager to help run their social and development programmes. At this stage I did not even know that this centre existed.

The job description seemed interesting. I would be able to do something challenging, helping people overcome all sorts of problems in their lives, based at the same time on Christian faith and ethos. The Centre dealt with addiction, mental health problems and poverty, and tried to help people who fell victim to any of these to find their feet again through counselling and support. As I was by now quite bored with the repetitive work at the call centre and saw no real future prospects there, I decided to apply for the position.

The two-phase interviews were to be held at the buildings adjacent to the cathedral and I was faced with an interview panel of about six people from the management committee, including the Dean of the cathedral and a Sister, the co-ordinator of the Cathedral Centre.

Though I have had endless experience in recruiting, no doubt a valuable asset when being the interviewee, this was once more a new and difficult situation for me. What would they make of me? I could not hide my past, even if I wanted to. After all, my excellent references referred to someone called Paul and yet here was I, Paula, answering all the questions. It went well until the very end when I was already leaving the room and the Sister asked one last and pertinent question. She wanted to know how I would cope with it when one of the clients would call me by some disparaging name—referring to my gender status. It was a most valid question and as I said in truth, I will only know when it happens, but I am strong and I will be able to deal with it.

Before the second interview I was offered and took the opportunity to work a few hours in the Centre. To be honest it was a bit scary at first, and I don't even mean the clients, though they too could be a little scary at times. No, it was the premises themselves. In my job at the call-centre I was working in a modern building with sunlight flooding in from all sides and here I was in an often stifling basement, where you could barely tell what was happening outside.

Meeting my possible future co-workers, volunteers and clients meant yet again more heart-in-mouth moments. I wondered if anyone on this first occasion would make some smart remark and ridicule me. But it went well and I got a first glimpse of what would be involved. Even from this short experience it was clear that it would never be dull or boring.

I was told that there were 26 applications for jobs and am happy to say I was successful, and was taken on with another girl by the name of Martina to fill the two vacancies. Though I had lots of managerial experience, nothing really particularly qualified me for this specific role and yet after my very first day I knew that I could do this work and wanted to do it well. On that first day a young guy, let's call him Richard, took an overdose of heroin and he fell into an almost comatose state. We laid him on one of the seats and I remember sitting there with his head on my lap, trying to check for vital signs. We could no longer feel a pulse and his pupils were like pin-pricks. He seemed to be slipping away. An ambulance had already been called, but in the meantime I sat there just speaking to him, holding him, praying for him and stifling my own tears. Yes, he was an addict, but I could just see a human being in trouble, in need of help, and I felt a compassion that surprised even me.

Richard made it; he returned once in a while and I always loved to see him as he reminded me of that first really challenging situation and how I coped with it. It was like a sign telling me that I could do this work well and that I would be able to search for the humanity behind the broken facades, the broken lives. I have learned that behind every addict or person with mental health problems there is usually a sad story; of bereavement, of relationship breakdowns, of neglect, of cruelty or abuse, and so often just a lack of love.

It may just be that there is a natural affinity for me to work with people on the margins, as I too have in some ways been forced to live on the margins of mainstream society.

This does not mean that the job was easy. Whatever the reasons for their addictions or mental problems and however hard you try to see their good side, some clients' behaviour can at times be abhorrent. You still have to run this kind of centre by upholding basic rules of conduct, which could at times lead to difficult and potentially dangerous situations. It could also be very frustrating to see clients you thought were heading in the right direction slipping backwards into addiction or errant behaviour. But every now and then, we did manage to get someone's life back on track and that alone was good reward for the work we tried to do.

Particularly difficult for me was the fact that certain individuals were quite willing to prey on the more vulnerable clients who used the Centre and that as a result some vulnerable people who needed our services most were frightened away. We did our best to prevent this, but of course had little chance of intervention outside.

There were always fundamental questions exercising my mind as well. If all such centres did not exist, no doubt some of the Centre users would be forced to take more responsibility for their own lives, but no doubt the most vulnerable and incapable people would go under. There is therefore a need for such centres for a core of people, who really haven't got the most basic skills to survive without help, but there is also a substantial number of people who use places like that as a convenience for cheap food and other services and even abuse the presence of such places for illegal activities in the vicinity.

But as I said, it was never boring, although much of the work could be mundane, such as the laundry or food preparation and serving. There was endless opportunity for engaging with people to offer them help and hope for the future. For me personally it also enabled me to put my considerable challenges over the past years into perspective, measured against the terrible situation many of our homeless clients found themselves in. Then I could say, there but for the grace of God go I. I am fortunate not to have an addictive streak and have never been tempted to escape my problems through drink or drugs or gambling.

And with regards to my own person, I was honest with people from the outset and if anyone asked me that question, which happened a couple of times, I told them the truth about my past gender transition. As the clients spoke among themselves, I could take it that all the regulars knew about this. Although there were a few isolated incidents, where someone I had to ask to leave for misdemeanours shouted some gender related insults at me. I coped with these incidents by not reacting, and hiding my pain.

There is absolutely no regret about my decision to have taken on this challenging work and I was so pleased at discovering such strong female traits of care and compassion within myself. I hoped to continue this work as an expression also of my growing faith.

Then in the summer of 2004 I had a pleasant interlude on a singles holiday in northern Cyprus with a bunch of really nice people. This gave me necessary respite from our demanding work environment.

It was my first real holiday as Paula; northern Cyprus is a pleasant though of course troubled territory divided from the Greek part of Cyprus. We were a group of about ten women and seven men; it was very pleasant and I was totally accepted as one of the crowd. It was really great to be able to go away as the person I now was, and to start creating new memories for my new life. Two significant incidents stand out for me from this holiday.

Most of us used to sunbathe and swim at the hotel pool, with only a few walking down to the small shingle beach occasionally. One day I found myself all alone there as a few had gone to get some lunch at the beach restaurant and I was sunbathing topless and struggling to get some suntan oil onto my back while lying on my stomach. Suddenly there was a male voice behind me offering to help me with the oil. I don't know what I was thinking, but I just reached the bottle behind me without even looking at the stranger. He proceeded swiftly to oil my back, and just as swiftly his hands were wandering all over my breasts. It wasn't his cheekiness which surprised me, but rather my reaction. Instead of instantly reprimanding him, I gasped at the sensation of having a stranger massaging me. It took a few moments of heavy breathing before I came to my senses and told him to stop. While I hadn't seen him, he might have been a most handsome guy in my imagination, but when I looked around he was a rather potbellied Turk gesticulating with broken English to the hotel and then writing his room number in the sand with obvious intent.

If his English had been a little better, and his belly a little smaller, well I might have been tempted. I realised that it had been a long time since someone had wanted me in this way, and that I had been well and truly starved of physical relations with another human being. But here I was, being propositioned by a man, who saw me as I wanted to be seen; as a woman.

I have deliberately not made much reference to sexuality in my story, because Gender Dysphoria is a problem of Gender Identification and is not directly related to sexuality. Gender is about who you are, and sexuality is about who you love.

When I started hormone treatment, receiving the testosterone suppressors and oestrogen, they quite quickly started to have an effect on my sexual appetite, and performance. The male function is quickly impaired, and after a while the prolonged use can have an effect on sexual orientation.

My sexual preference is still women, though I would now describe myself as bi-sexual. My interest in men is at best ambiguous. But on that occasion, as I lay sunbathing, it was the fact that I was being treated as a woman that made me hesitate before stopping him and declining his invitation.

\*\*\*

On another occasion we went to a late-night beach barbecue. It was warm and the sea in the small, secluded bay looked calm and inviting. We had some tasty Turkish food; all sorts of kebabs, and the wine flowed freely. After a while some of the group decided to strip off and get into the water, and given the atmosphere of joviality, I couldn't resist, and discreetly stripped off my bikini and followed the others into the water. These were very special moments for me—the warm water lit by silvery moonlight dancing on the little waves gave a real sense of magic, and would give me fond memories for years to come. But more importantly, it felt at that moment that I, Paula, had arrived; I felt so at peace with myself, swimming slowly out to sea, feeling every part of my body tingling with the caressing salt water. It had taken me more than 50 years to feel so at ease with my body. It was a time I will never forget. But all too soon the holiday was over.

\*\*\*

Six months after I had started at the Cathedral Centre there were a lot of changes in our management team, but we built up a good sense of team spirit with the new team and I can say that I never had a problem with going to work.

But just as I had found a period of calm in my life, events unfolded to put my future in peril once more. First the Sister at the Centre, the person I learned so much from over the first eighteen months, decided to leave and return to Ireland to aid her ageing and ill parents. This led to new stress for our staff team, most of whom were still new in their jobs. Then my colleague, who it had been such a pleasure to work with, decided to leave as well as she found it hard to cope with the occasional violence associated with the job.

My decision to apply for the co-ordinator's job, supported by my colleagues, was quickly made redundant by unfolding events. After 15 years of existence just one phone call from the bishop to the Sister informed us that the Centre would be closed within weeks. We were all distraught and dismayed, not only at the decision, but the way in which it was made without any consultation or sufficient time to move to alternative premises.

Clients who had used the Centre for years, loyal volunteers who had given such commitment though they were often frail and in advancing years, and the paid staff members whose livelihoods were now in peril, were distraught in equal measure. We then tried frantically to find an alternative location. Letters were written, presentations made, the local media highlighted our case, but it proved too difficult and no one came forward to offer a viable alternative. The Centre finally closed its doors that February. It appears that the church allowed a valuable service for the most vulnerable people to fall victim to their development and restructuring plans. Those on the margins of society have no voice and will be marginalised even more.

The paid staff members were awarded a fair redundancy package and for me a frustrating job search started again. Though I sent many detailed applications for positions I was well capable of doing, I got no positive replies for weeks. Nobody seems to want you if you are the wrong side of 50, irrespective of your skills and your commitment. I eventually found a temporary placement working with ex-offenders, but I wish I was back at the Cathedral because I felt that I understood those people who were living on the margins of society, just like I was forced to do.

However, I must look forward. I hope the future will give me the opportunity to once more find a challenging and rewarding role, where I can employ the many skills gained over the years in my diverse roles on both sides of the gender division.

The trouble is that while much good legislation has been introduced over recent years (The Sex Discrimination Regulations 1999 and Employment Equality Regulations Act 2006), insidious discrimination based on age and gender persists, and only a change of attitude rather than a change of laws can allow women to play a truly equal role in society—especially transgendered women.

# CONCLUSION

Why write this book? You might well ask. Of course I have asked myself too. At the beginning, the main motivation was to write as a form of self-therapy, a way of dealing with the enormous pain and anguish I felt at my parting from my family. I wanted to hold on to the raw emotions I felt as events unfolded, but it also gave me a sense of purpose—as long as I hadn't finished my story I would resist the, at times, strong urges to self destruct. Yes, in those darkest days I stood more than once at my 15th storey window and contemplated a rapid descent to oblivion, an end to my pain and my loneliness. But the memories of my sister's suicide and just one phrase from her final note: 'To tell you the truth it's failure, because it's giving up on life,' made it clear to me that I could not put my family through that anguish. I know that I am not a quitter. The gift of life must not be wasted, even if it can be a cross to bear at times.

I also wrote from a strong sense of history. Maybe because I was uprooted early in my life, I always wanted to know my roots, put stories to the faded sepia faces in old black and white photographs of my now dead relatives; most of their lives are largely blank and hidden from me, and so I wanted to leave a personal record for my own descendants; of what it is like to feel compelled to live on the margins, in the no-man's land between the genders.

By writing about my experiences, I wanted to show what it means to be transgendered at the beginning of the 21st century. As difficult as many parts of my life's journey have been, it has also been an extraordinary experience—living in different societies, experiencing life from different gender viewpoints—a unique opportunity given to few.

Also, as my writing progressed, it felt like an act of atonement; by allowing my sins of the past to be exposed, I hope for forgiveness. There are moments and acts of betrayal in my past I am not proud of, but it has taken all of these experiences to make me the person I am today. Successful lives are not built by never experiencing failures, but by accepting responsibility for these failures and then drawing the right conclusions from them to build upon and so allow each failure to become a stepping stone to success.

I sincerely hope that my story will facilitate an act of mutual forgiveness with all the people whose lives I have touched. My own wounds are no longer dressed in anger or hatred, and it is with serenity that I can say that I hate no one. Though I can't easily forget some of the things that seriously impacted my life, I find solace in forgiveness.

Then of course I hope that my story will make even a small and hopefully positive contribution to the lives of other transpeople, by showing that we are in almost every respect no different from most other people; we have the same aspirations of freedom, friendship and love, the right to be ourselves and to advance our careers and personal prosperity, which may mean either material or spiritual prosperity, or both.

Of course there are bad eggs in every basket and some are put there through ignorance and fear. Suffering from Gender Identity Disorder can still lead to isolation and disaffection with society, resulting in some transpeople ending up in prostitution, addiction, depression and still too often an early death. These examples are then eagerly picked up by the gutter press to reinforce negative images, which in turn further alienate us from the mainstream community. We are not asking for a special deal—just to be treated like everyone else, given the same rights, and of course allowed to take on the same responsibilities.

This is the 21st century; it can no longer be the age of leper colonies. We should be enlightened enough to see human diversity as enriching and not as threatening. There are many people in the UK and Ireland suffering with syndromes that make them different. Most are used to being stared at with sympathetic curiosity. Transgendered people may also be stared at with curiosity if they are not lucky enough to pass successfully in their gender role. Here though there is little sympathy, because even though these groups suffer from recognised conditions, in the case of the transgendered the perception of the public is still that theirs is a lifestyle choice. This often leads to marginalisation and a lowered average life-expectancy, not for sound medical reasons, but because the burdens and stress of social exclusion become too heavy to bear for many.

No doubt we all ask ourselves 'What if?' from time to time. There are so many crossroads in our lives where either different circumstances or decisions would have led to totally different lives. What if I had the proper information in my puberty to seek help? I cry at times for the young girl within who never lived. Indeed I might have had a better life if I had been able to transition earlier on in life, but then again I would not have my children, whom I love dearly. Then there would have been no one to carry on my genes.

All the *what ifs* in the past are useless and we can only make the best of what we have got now and try to choose wisely so we won't have to ask more *what ifs* tomorrow.

My book is the final removal of the endless lie I felt forced to live. Even as I write this book I am aware of the pain this causes all around. Recently my first grandchild, a beautiful boy, was christened in a rural church in Ireland, but I could be there only in spirit. I could not be there as it would have caused too much controversy. My son was filled with anguish and was troubled, and my heart went out to him. If he had asked me to be there, others who do not know about me would not or could not have come.

So what is it like to be me: a transwoman, exiled in the UK? As a Christian, I am familiar with Jesus' teaching through parables; often he talks of himself as the good shepherd and sees us as his often wayward flock of sheep. When I think back on my days in Africa I remember often not being able to tell between sheep and goats. There would be a flock of sheep with an odd goat or two running with them. All would look too lean and, covered in the same dust of the local parched earth, they would become almost indistinguishable.

Well, I think of myself as a little goat, trying hard, very hard, to belong to the flock of sheep. The little goat is allowed to run with the sheep, tolerated among the flock, accepted even, yet never quite a complete part of it. When evening comes and the sheep settle down together, bleating quietly to each other, there would pipe up the similar and yet also different sound of this little goat, and because it sounds different it would often not let its voice be heard because it was self-conscious of that different sound.

I guess no two transpeople can tell the same story. There would be differences based on background and other life experiences, but there would also be many similarities. A few can manage to stay in their familiar environment and find strong support from family and friends. A few are so convincing that they can start anew in new surroundings, eradicating their different gender past from their life story, though that amounts to once more having to live a lie. Many would be like me—unwilling or unable to make the fresh start without any disclosure of the past, as it would mean disowning family and loved ones, the same loved ones who on the other hand are often ready to deny my existence. Not totally disowned, but still preferred at a safe distance.

As another transsexual friend recently said to me, we have only two choices. Either we live on a knife's edge or we live in a fish bowl! Those who have transitioned and live in new surroundings and do not share their history constantly live on a knife edge, fearing discovery and disclosure at any moment. Those who are very open about their gender transition live in a fish bowl, often feeling that those who know look at them in a particular scrutinising way, maybe to tick off the flaws, check for giveaways, and then again a lot of that may just be self-consciousness.

All this leads to great difficulty in building new relationships. Though I have always found women to be more understanding and compassionate, there still is an often invisible barrier to finding total admission to their close circles, to be just one of the girls. Maybe it is born of my own insecurity.

The transition procedure and treatment meant that the testosterone-driven desire I had for women in the past is now gone, replaced by a womanly desire to be loved simply as a woman. As for men; well, every time I meet someone I like, I am faced with the same dilemma: Do I just let it run, enjoy the moment, or do I disclose my secret at the first possible chance? If I don't, I may have some fun, and I may even fall in love, but love is based on trust and trust can't be built on lies.

On the other hand, if I do disclose my gender transition, most men will run, because they cannot cope with such a situation; they start asking themselves silly questions about their own sexuality. And for the remainder that might stay, I am again the one left unsure; do they stay because they truly want Paula, the attractive, interesting woman, or do they have some kinky fascination for transsexuals? Is it Paula the cute sheep among the other sheep or Paula the exotic goat they want?

It leaves the future very uncertain and yet, as hard as the journey has been and still is, there are no regrets about embarking on my transition. At least I am who I was meant to be. There are regrets however, that it is still necessary, even now in this day and age, to pay such a huge price socially, financially and emotionally for being born with a female mind in a male shell.

Though I have by and large finished transition in a physical sense, grudgingly accepting my voice as less than perfect—a fact I am regularly reminded of when using the telephone—it's on Wednesdays that Paula, the emotional woman, is forced to confront the remnants of her unwanted biological past during long sessions of facial electrolysis. It robs me of a whole day of my week, because I feel raw in my face and raw in my heart, because I still cannot close that chapter for good. Yes, it is easier to have Gender Reassignment Surgery than to get rid of the facial hair.

Gender Transition is still a most difficult journey and though I have come through the physical procedures with few visible scars, some of the emotional scars can only truly heal when I manage to build meaningful new relationships.

Every now and then there is a little incident which causes so much pain, even if the person causing the incident is blissfully unaware of their ignorance. Luckily the last such incident is by now more than a year ago. While browsing in a boutique a guy stopped me on the way out to flog me a badge for some children's charity. As I was chatting to him while searching in my purse for a pound coin he said: 'Excuse me, if you don't mind me asking, were you by any chance ever a man before?'

Yes, I do mind you asking! Something, very possibly my voice, had awoken his curiosity, but why do people not think about the silly questions they ask? If I just happened to be a regular woman with a slightly husky voice, or whatever caused his curiosity, would I not be highly offended to be mistaken for a bloke? And if indeed I am transsexual, but very obviously presenting in female gender, do I really want to be seen as anything other than female? Questions like this are like a kick in the proverbial crotch. Though I managed to answer this fellow's question in an even voice with a false smile on my face, inside I was crying.

You go home then, self-confidence undermined, scrutinising every facet of make-up or clothes to find what tripped you up. An incident like this can agitate, frustrate and hurt for hours, or even days. I cried myself to sleep that night, while thinking about what I could do if I had the resources; have my face ripped up again, nose once more stream-lined, jaw broken and reset, eye-brow bones planed and honed, vocal cords spliced in the hope of even a slim chance of that elusive feminine voice, the lowest ribs ripped out, all kinds of pain and agony to become more indistinguishable from all the other women, to be anonymous in the crowd and to belong and yes, at the same time to gain a few years to make up for all the best years of womanhood I could never have.

Life without love is most difficult and life without friends isn't worth living. It is only when I have fully left the no-man's land between the genders by taking my place as the woman I was meant to be, endorsed by new, meaningful friendships and hopefully crowned by finding love once more, that I can say my life's journey is complete.

Nobody can be certain of their future—all we can do is draw from the experiences of our past, striving to live each day as the first day of the rest of our lives, and to live them well. And as long as there is hope, everything is still possible.

# LOOT

## INSIDE THE WORLD OF STOLEN ART

### BY THOMAS MCSHANE
### WITH DARY MATERA

Thomas McShane is one of the world's foremost authorities on the art theft business and in *Loot* he recounts some of his most thrilling cases as he matched wits with Mafia mobsters and smooth criminals.

Covering his 36 years as an FBI Agent, the author brings us on a thrilling ride through the underworld of stolen art and historical artefacts as he donned his many disguises and aliases to chase down $900 million worth of stolen art pieces. In the end, he always got his man, but the way in which he did it each time is told with great energy and imagination.

He worked on high profile cases all over the world, including the Beit heist in Ireland. From Rembrandts robbed in Paris to van Goghs vanishing in New York, McShane's tale is one of great adventure, told with surprising humour.

*The Thomas Crown Affair* meets *Donnie Brasco* in this story of a truly extraordinary life.

To order this book go to www.maverickhouse.com